ACTIVITY IN THE PRIMARY SCHOOL

# Drama in the Primary School

**Activity in the Primary School**

General Editor: *Don Buckland*

*Titles in the Series*

Games and Sports *by W. M. Wise*
Swimming *by David Morris*
Dance *by Peter Lofthouse*
Drama in the Primary School *by Janet Goodridge*
Gymnastics *by Don Buckland*
Reading *by Peter Horner*
Using the Urban Environment *by Michael Williams & Steven Bell*
Art *by Seymour Jennings*
Music *by Muriel Hart*

# Drama in the Primary School

*by*

Janet Goodridge

H·E·B

Heinemann Educational Books
London

Heinemann Educational Books Ltd
LONDON EDINBURGH MELBOURNE AUCKLAND TORONTO
SINGAPORE HONG KONG KUALA LUMPUR
IBADAN NAIROBI JOHANNESBURG
LUSAKA NEW DELHI KINGSTON

ISBN 0 435 80604 1


First published 1970
Reprinted 1971
Reprinted (with corrections) 1973, 1975, 1977

Published by Heinemann Educational Books Ltd
48 Charles Street, London W1X 8AH
Printed Offset Litho and bound in Great Britain by
Cox & Wyman Ltd, London, Fakenham and Reading

# Introduction to the Series

Young children have an instinctive delight in movement. They respond with pleasure to a natural urge to run, jump, throw, climb and dance. The teacher who sets out to develop this energy into useful and creative activities can expect his pupils to be enthusiastic and responsive. The experience is likely to be particularly rewarding for both teacher and class, for during the period of development covered by this series of handbooks, the growth of skill, awareness, versatility and confidence is astounding. The teacher does not need to be an expert performer or to hold specialist qualifications in physical education. In fact, one hopes that the children in our Infant and Junior Schools will continue to be taught by those who are first and foremost experts in the teaching of children. In Middle Schools a qualified teacher who can serve as the power house for physical education will be needed, although it is to be hoped that he will not adopt the traditional role of the specialist. His task will be to inspire, enthuse, co-ordinate and guide the rest of the staff in their work with their classes, and, by virtue of his own personal ability and example, to set the tempo of the extra-curricular programme.

*Moving and Growing* drew attention to the ways in which children learn – by repetition, by exploration, through creation, through contact with each other, with the teacher and other adults. Now teachers create learning situations according to the nature of each individual child and the stage he has reached. Planning, organization and knowledge are necessary, and this series of handbooks sets out to provide this help. They offer suggestions for work in a balanced programme of physical education for the stages of education suggested by the Plowden Report, i.e. the first eight years of compulsory schooling from five years to twelve plus.

Drama is included in the series, in addition to Games, Gymnastics, Swimming and Dance, because of its obvious links with movement, and its value as an activity whereby so much of the work in the Primary

School may be integrated. It is not suggested that all five aspects of physical education will be covered concurrently. It might be more effective to deal intensively with one or two activities for a concentrated block of time. We do suggest, however, that all aspects should be included in a balanced programme for each stage of primary education.

The tremendous growth of new subjects and new approaches in the Primary School in recent years has made very great demands upon the teacher. Time for planning and preparation is precious, and there is a danger that physical education will either be seen merely as a chance for letting off steam, or will be squeezed out altogether by the pressure of other work. It is hoped that this series will enable the teacher to see the subject as contributing to the process of education as a whole; as another way of assisting the development of people.

January, 1970. DON BUCKLAND

*General Editor*

# Preface

My work in Drama has developed from many sources which it would be difficult to trace in full. I must, however record my debt to colleagues, students and children with whom I have worked. I wish especially to thank Miss Lisa Ullman (Director of the Laban Art of Movement Centre), Mr Peter Slade, Miss Geraldine Stephenson, Miss Leila Davies, Dr Dorothy Madden (Chairman, Dance Department, University of Maryland), Mr George Brandt (Drama Department, University of Bristol) and Miss Elsie Pracy for her valuable help with this handbook, notably in the sections on Louis Braille, My Town, North Sea Floods, Columbus, Indians, Mary Kingsley, Energy and Movement of the Sun.

I am grateful to the following for permission to print children's work which they initiated; Barbara Phillips (poems by children at Darton High School, nr. Barnsley, Yorks on p. 52); M. A. Braybrooks (play on p. 142 by children at Gloucester Road Primary School, London); R. S. Ronan (play on p. 155 by children at Henry Maynard Junior School, Walthamstow, London), and to Edith Erridge for the play and piece of writing on p. 44. I would also like to thank Henry Metcalfe for the photographs used on the cover.

JANET GOODRIDGE

# Contents

*No one passes through life scatheless. The world has many sour noises; the body is an open target. . . . yet even so, each of us, one time or another can ride a white horse, can have rings on our fingers and bells on our toes, and if we keep our senses open to the scents, sounds and sights all around us, we shall have music wherever we go.*
Sean O'Casey (in an interview two weeks before his death)

*Everyone is talented. If he is deeply interested in his work, every healthy man has a deep capacity for developing the creative energies in his nature.*
Lazlo Moholy–Nagy (Bauhaus teacher)

# Chapter 1: Introduction

This handbook aims to provide some suggestions for Drama in Primary Schools and in particular to assist teachers in the selection of appropriate material. Drama in the Primary School is a continuation and extension of the dramatic expression seen in the play of young children. This has its origin in a response, a response to something felt, seen, heard or smelt. Observation will have been an important part of the activity which, however, may appear to have little to do with real experiences. Exaggeration and distortion occur: the dramatic play is an expression of what is going on in the child's mind. Adult anger, for instance, is often played out with dolls or younger children as much sterner than it was in real life. In dramatic play the child is involved in an imaginative situation. Objects are used as symbols for absent persons and things, and sometimes disguise is worn as part of the dramatic activity.

With dramatic play, physical development and mental growth are interwoven trends in the child's general play activity. So too, in school life, should drama be considered with other activities. It can be the pivot or subsidiary in Centre of Interest work. Drama is action, movement, a form of physical, including vocal, expression. Therefore it has a near relationship with physical education (hence its inclusion in this series). It is also important to consider English, art, craft and music in relation to drama. Some would say that it is dependent on these and other disciplines such as history, geography and religion for its content and existence, that in the Primary School, drama is a process, an activity rather than a subject. Children's drama should certainly not be a diluted form of adult drama or theatre; it has skills, techniques of its own.

It is easy to make pretentious claims for drama in education. To quote from an article on the subject by John Pick[1], we can be guilty of contributing to 'the flood of indisciplined claims for drama teaching which washes over lecturers in education and even laps up on the shores of the text-book industry'. However, if our teaching is to be interesting and effective we must examine aims, purpose and the hopefully anticipated value of what we do. Drama interests us because of the constantly changing characters and situation. This interrelation is only to an extent predictable and we see how man deals with the choices open to him and with creative and destructive opportunities. In pursuance of this interest, what areas of experience are being offered to the child? Movement, speech, movement with speech. Which specific aspect of any one of these? What is the drama experience? Drama shares with other subjects on the school timetable opportunities for physical, emotional, mental, individual and social activities of a creative nature.

'Improvisation' is a term often used to describe school drama. It generally means acting on a given idea or theme without forethought or outside direction, and much of the drama in the Primary School should be of this kind. The work should also include polished or worked-on improvisations and playmaking which requires forethought. Formal drama does not warrant a place in the Primary School curriculum, meaning as it usually does, the reading, study and critical analysis of dramatic literature, or rehearsal and production of ready-made scripts. 'Mime' is also an adult art when it is taught as a set, traditional vocabulary of expressive movement. In the sense of acting freely without words it is of course the basis of drama and fundamental in drama teaching.

'Dance Drama' is frequently included in the school drama syllabus. The principles of dance drama derive partly from dance, partly from drama. The dramatic elements of character situation and action are wholly translated into dance expression, mimetic or symbolic. Dance makes more obvious use of regular, metric rhythm, locomotion and elevation than drama, and exaggeration of normal gestures, with turns and changes of level.

What is the function of the teacher? Whether drama is fully creative or not depends not only on the children and the material but also on the teacher and teaching methods. It is possible to be creative in formal and informal drama. However, encouraging creativity in the children does not mean that the teacher relinquishes control of the class. What it does mean is that he avoids dominating the work. 'Drama in many schools fails in development through excessive domination by the teacher. No real exploration of any area of human experience can be achieved by children or young people when the area to be explored, and in many cases the manner in which it is to be explored, have been arbitrarily imposed.'[2]

It is necessary for the teacher to provide situations which challenge the intelligence, efforts, and energies of the children. To quote the Plowden Report on the English teacher's job, 'She cannot continue to draw indefinitely on the children's haphazard experience of living; she must always feed in new experience to the child, which should be presented so as to affect him deeply and touch him through the life of the senses, the emotions and the imagination.' See also Margaret Mead's discussion of Manus society which suggests the need of giving children something upon which to exercise their imagination.[3] The teacher should value the opportunity drama gives for energy release and see that there is plenty of interesting, absorbing work for the children to do. He should be prepared to modify his ideas according to class response and avoid embellishing, altering, 'making more interesting', if irrelevant to the child's intentions. He should know when to avoid breaking continuity and be able to judge when to bring a piece of work to an end.

One of the most important functions of the teacher is that of observer. He needs to be able to discern what is significant in whatever the child does in relation to his present abilities, his growth and development. He needs to see that drama does not remain an opportunity for indulgence in personal characteristics. Drama is not there to help the bully practise his bullying. The child should be helped to consider and attempt many roles.

The teacher has to watch for over-excitement in the class leading to lack of control. Drama needs self-control and self-discipline and this is one way of justifying its existence on the school timetable. 'The problem of getting rid of undesirable repression can be attacked by specific methods. Of these, the method of encouraging self-expression through creative activity which is both free and self-disciplined is probably the most important,' writes Dr Julian Huxley in his essay, 'Education as a Social Function.'[4]

As teachers, we are helping the child to perceive, to think and to express. We are developing his sensitivity and let us hope we are beginning to help him cope sensibly with the suffering and awareness of suffering which increased sensitivity can lead to. In short, 'The teacher must see with the eyes of a child but direct him towards being an adult.'[5]

BOOK REFERENCES

1. John Pick, 'A Little Food for Thought', *English in Education*, Vol. 1, No. 3.
2 *Drama Survey*, H.M.S.O.
3 Margaret Mead, *Growing Up in New Guinea*, Penguin Books.
4. J. Huxley, *Man in the Modern World*, Chatto & Windus.
5 *The Story of a School*, H.M.S.O.

# Chapter 2: Children and Drama

*10th March*: Yesterday I was put in the play. I am Thryn's servant....
*11th March*: Last night my mother helped me in making me a dress for the play. The belt is a dressing gown cord. I made my shoes at home but I have only enough tape for one shoe.
*13th March*: Yesterday I painted the collar, sleeves, and bottom of my dress blue. My dad and mum are going to see the play and we are going to act it in front of Miss C (the headmistress).
*16th March*: T M is Loki in our play and he has to change into a bird. Some girls and Miss H are making wings. It is about finished now. He has a black cap and a paper beak. I think he looks very much like a bird.
*17th March*: I made the plaits but I could not get one finished. So I took it home and finished it there. I did not know I liked acting so much. I think I will become an actress. I don't think it's hard work in fact I think it's all fun.
*18th March*: Yesterday just before we did our show my shoe tore. My dad is going to make me another pair out of felt. I have a stocking to cover up my hair. I will be wearing plaits made from raffia and as I have dark hair I have to cover it. Most people say that my hair is black. Actually it is dark brown. Also it is naturally curly.

Barbara, aged 9.

The success of drama depends chiefly on the interest and experience of the teacher and his relationship with the class. Why does he wish to introduce or encourage drama? What are his aims? Success also depends on suitable choice of material, partly influenced by the teacher's interests, partly influenced by the following:

1. The age and/or stage of development, characteristics and interests of the children. As in any subject, in drama the teacher needs to estimate the child's potentialities and abilities, and to demand work and behaviour which are relevant to them at any particular stage of

growth. By watching and evaluating the children's stages of development the teacher can select new challenges which will continue to stimulate progress.

2. The particular needs of the class, physical, mental, emotional and social.
3. The ability of the class: in understanding, movement and speech. It is important to start well within these abilities. The success of drama also depends on the quality of the children's thinking and creative response.
4. The previous training of the class (whether formal, informal, etc.). Are they used to partner or group work?
5. The use of the space available: hall or classroom, etc.
6. The use of other facilities available: rostra, record player.

It is hoped that the following brief notes in chart form will help the teacher to consider 1, 2, and 3 in more detail. Only the teacher can find out what interests the children, and he must begin, though not end, with this. There can be no hard and fast rules to propose concerning what to do at different ages and how to do it. Children vary in their rate of growth and development. Much depends on environment, on the degree and quality of communication between parents and children, and on the child's ability to form ideas from his experiences. However, there are distinct stages in growth and development, and by examining the characteristics, interests and needs, even very generally at any given stage, the teacher can go a long way towards providing himself with a basis from which to select and develop suitable drama experience. In the Introduction and the following brief summary I suggest that the instinct for and practice of drama exists in children without any formal teaching. This should be borne in mind when considering the function of the teacher.

Some of the points made are about beginning drama in the Primary School, but characteristics and needs of the five-year-old are equally applicable to beginners in drama at any age. For instance, I have seen thirty-five to forty-year-old men, beginners in drama, behaving in ways identical to the five-year-old, and needing similar opportunities and techniques from the teacher. Given percussion instruments to use for the first time they leapt around the room with insistent beating, getting faster and faster.

## INFANTS

| *General Characteristics* | *Interests* | *Movement* | *Language* | *Brief comments on drama work in school* |
|---|---|---|---|---|
| Needs, invites and accepts guidance. Likes to do a thing his own way, but also likes to conform and to please adults. Is curious. Has difficulty in distinguishing between fantasy and reality. Gradually draws nearer to world of reality and laws; withdraws from fantasy, although fantasy is still present. | Likes to have possessions. Collects things. Interests centre on mother and himself. Lives in the present. Imitative play – shop, house, hospital. Interest is in *doing*. | Is poised and controlled. Marked interest in stunts and skills. Proud of dexterity. Very active. Can maintain a position. Can achieve simple movement pathways. Enjoys active outdoor games. Explores physically – e.g. puddle splashing, climbing, going down slides. In movement and drama takes pleasure in understanding 'big', 'small' and 'grow'. | The aim is to assist confidence in speaking. Speech should flow from activity and from having something to communicate. Do not expect to hear everything that is said. By now vocabulary should be adequate for him to get what he wants, but still limited for expression of feeling and thoughts. | Use sounds as stimuli the child enjoys and wants to make. Can react to pulse, simple repetition, climax and de-climax in accompaniment. Creative, exploratory teaching is required. Avoid audience for this age group and for as long as possible hereafter. Help needed at right stage in distinguishing between fantasy and reality: fantasy becomes imagination and conscious pretence. The first stage is being an individual within a group, all working at the same time. Likes 'being' things. By the end of the first year some children reach the stage where they do not want to be everything in story playing so they wait for 'their characters' as the story progresses. Avoid solos, have groups even of single characters. Keep the stories short but have plenty of occupational movement content for the characters. From approx. 6 years onwards partner work is possible – action and reaction. At first it is easier to work with a partner of one's own choosing. From 6½ years onwards group work should be well established. Leaders emerge. The sense of a progressive sequence develops – by the end of this first stage different areas of the room can represent different places in the story play for journeys (see Chapter 4 and pp. 59–65, 73–80). |

## LOWER JUNIORS

| *General Characteristics* | *Interests* | *Movement* | *Language* | *Brief comments on drama work in school* |
|---|---|---|---|---|
| A few children are ready for individual parts. Increasingly able to work with partners. More stable play groups or gangs exist – although membership may change during the week. Leaders emerge. Beginning of real co-operative play if children have had the chance to progress through the earlier stages of individual play, if they have gained skill in the use of tools and materials, and if they have had time to get adjusted to other children, and are sufficiently mature to be able to give sustained attention to a task. Still enjoy repetition. Later more real talent for leadership shows, and increasing interest in adults and other cultures. Begins to have special friends. Sense of fairness develops. Enjoys variety and humour. increasingly matter-of-fact. | Enjoys making books on interests. Has crazes and hobbies and personal collections. Likes manipulating things, sometimes puppets and puppet theatres very popular. Interested in magic and tricks. Girls enjoy domesticity and tidying. Increasingly enjoys visiting places; e.g., zoos. Likes map-making and making of own games and rules. Also later classifies and arranges his collections more efficiently. | Can maintain a position longer. Develops a liking for stunts and feats of daring. Follow-my-leader is popular. Elementary phrasing flow, and direct and flexible movement can be clearly distinguished. Increased grace and speed in movement. | Can reason, consider and choose more easily. Improvised speech should be well established. Likes myths, legends, books on trades, occupations army, etc. at approximately 8 years. Likes to argue, dramatize. Encourage clear, easily heard speech; deaf characters can be portrayed to help this. Can write well by now. Enjoys stories such as those by Grimm, Hans Anderson. Likes surprises in a story. Likes monsters, dragons. Old Testament stories can be used. | Drama work can appear lacking in full movement due to tendency to live through it mentally and ritualize. As children mature this desire to ritualize fades and the movement becomes more fully expressive in dramatic context. Can cope with more detail. Still needs teacher as narrator, but will outgrow this soon. Can use their own experiences in drama also continue everyday situations. Development of the use of the floor. They can still all be everything although a few will be ready for individual parts. (See chapters 4, 5 and relevant sections in 6). |

## UPPER JUNIORS

| *General Characteristics* | *Interests* | *Movement* | *Language* | *Brief comments on drama work in school* |
|---|---|---|---|---|
| Self-motivation is stronger in this age group. Keeps himself busy. Has many friends. Enjoys team games. Accepts own role in the group. Very cooperative. Good partner work. Urgent. More critical, e.g. of parents. Impressionable. Persistent. Independent. Becoming ready to enter into other people's experiences and points of view. Gangs very noticeable at about 10 years. From 10–11 lasting personal friends. May be more relaxed. | Spying, hiding, frightening others. Making friends. Reading. Use of private codes. Prices of things. Geography of neighbourhood. About 9½ – historical sense and intelligent interest in History develops. From 10 years various hobbies, some now to be retained through life. | Use of body in activities and rhythms develops further. Tends to continue until exhausted. Movement skill and vocabulary considerably increases. Phrasing develops further, also clarity of gesture, shaping and body shape. Boys become stronger, wilder. | Speech should be very fluent. Can write quite long passages, and can invent endings. Enjoy stories about animals, high seas, travel, real adventure, explorers, treasure islands, King Arthur, jobs of work, jokes, guarding things. Considerable interest in history from 10 onwards. Still interested in myth and legend. Inventions in history are popular topics, also game hunters. From 11 we should be careful to encourage appropriate speech. At this stage children may be able to enjoy attempting different accents e.g. rough cockney, refined, foreign accents, inventing own gibberish language. | Needs plenty of activity. Enjoyment of fighting can be made use of (see chapter 5). Control develops: seen in slow movements as in sea or space and in the use of invisible heavy or outsize objects. More organized and confident use of space can be expected (acting areas and changes of level: rostra). Awareness of entries can begin although dramatic work should still be on the floor rather than on the stage. Changes of direction, focus, and awareness of 'near' and 'far' can be used more effectively. Use of sounds should continue though use of recorded music can increase. The children take more responsibility yet the teacher can give effective guidance to the older children. Richer characterization and deeper plot is required in drama as in stories. By approximately 8–9 years should be wanting to make up their own stories, plays. More awareness of division into scenes. By about 10 years, the children are acquiring the ability to select, and a sense of form is being achieved. From this period on, the children can be acting their own scripts and working on polished improvisations. From about 12 years onwards small amounts of scripted plays can be introduced if plays which have situations and characters of interest and relevance to the children can be found. Interest in TV and theatre arts begin to develop. (See Chapters 5, 6 and 7.) |

Whatever stage the class has reached, the teacher begins there and takes whatever the children offer, using it immediately in the class situation.

## Some questions to ask

This section is designed to help the teacher who has not attempted dramatic work before.

By considering questions such as these from time to time, the teacher can begin to assess the degree of involvement and progress of the children in their drama work.

1. *Children's interest*

Are they interested?
Are they asking questions?
Are they continuing drama work interest out of the classroom, out of school?
Do they bring things from home to show, discuss or use in drama?
Are they pleased to show their work to others?

2. *Physical abilities*

Is the child rigid or flexible? Has he adequate resilience and control in his movements?
Are there any body areas he could use better or more fully?
Does he have an increasing 'movement vocabulary', and an increasing awareness of movement possibilities?
Are the children using the space well? (i.e. not bunching, using changes of direction easily and without collision, etc.)
Does he have an increasing ability to improvise spontaneously and to formulate clearly?
Can he compose alone or with others a short movement or sequence?
Can he learn and remember a movement phrase?
Can he handle materials, objects in drama well? (The last four questions are more appropriate for seven-year-olds upwards.)

3. *Emotional expression/reactions*

Is he secure, stable/unstable/calm/tense/friendly/shy/anxious/self-confident?
Is he dependable/dependent?
Can he adapt easily to different stimuli?

4. *Relationship with others*
Does he play/talk easily with other children and adults?
Does he work more co-operatively, more sensitively with others than he used to?
Does he contribute to group work? (More appropriate for seven-year-olds upwards.)

5. *Initiative/ideas*
Do they show initiative?
Do they work with good concentration when alone or undirected?
Can they choose their activities and/or roles in drama work easily?
Are they absorbed in their drama work?
If signs of leadership are evident, how is this gained over other children? (More appropriate for seven-year-olds upwards.)

6. *Thought/language/listening and observing*
Is his use of words adequate or above average?
Can he talk easily with adults?
Does he follow spoken/written directions easily?
Can he listen with understanding?
Is he able to recognize, move to and make simple rhythms and/or tunes?
Are his powers of observation improving?

7. *Teacher's planning*
Are the children's physical, emotional, mental, creative and social needs being met in some measure by drama?
What opportunities have been given for extending experience in specific areas (such as movement, speech, dramatic genres)?
What has been learnt?

8. *Teaching Technique (for beginner teachers)*
Are we communicating with each other effectively? (I.e. am I using words the children understand?)
Am I able to gain class attention at any time by use of mutually understood sign or sound?
Could I improve my story telling, the use of my voice, the use of words? (E.g. I need at least five different words to convey a characteristic quality, e.g. firm strength: pull, heave, press, push, squash.)

Am I extending their vocabulary by my own use of words?

For the teacher, it is important to allow interest and skill in the subject to develop at a personal level, but without confusing this with the children's work, or imposing adult conventions on them, or allowing personal ideas for topics to become more important than they should.

Thus, as indicated in the Introduction, the teacher needs to consider carefully his own approach to the children's drama work. He should aim to discuss the work and work plans with the children, helping especially the older children to understand the what, how, and why of the activity and what is required of them in relation to it. Are they experiencing the pleasure that is to be derived from making things and are they gaining a sense of achievement? As for discipline problems, these are reduced if there is sufficient interest and therefore absorption in the work, plus a growing self-control and awareness of others.

Children need sufficient opportunity for exercising choice of activity in Drama. They also need to be 'stretched', that is, given sufficient challenge so that they can work and extend comprehension to their fullest extent. To help in this direction it is important that they be given sufficient time for exploration, thought, repetition, consolidation and conversation.

'Mistakes' can be turned to opportunities for learning, especially if one has a positive attitude to them so that apparent failure can be accepted and turned to good use. In drama a 'mistake' can so often be seen to be simply a different way of doing something which may in fact turn out to be a better way. For instance, a top-Junior class had a group of birds in their play. One bird overbalanced by 'mistake' and quickly righted itself but this was seen to be much more naturally bird-like than any other movement the group had tried. Result: the overbalancing and quickly righting was incorporated into the sequence. The teacher's sympathy with the children's difficulties should never be underestimated; they need help and encouragement as well as sufficient stimuli from the teacher.

Perhaps some aspects of dramatic activity are over-emphasized whilst others are even omitted. Children respond to variety and the teacher can learn to be conscious of the effect of different activities and movements, for example the value of calm work at the end of the lesson or period of drama experience. New ways of beginning lessons should be tried in order to elicit a fresh response and readiness for creative work.

It is worth checking that the equipment is suitably stored and easily accessible (e.g. is your record player/tape recorder so placed that you can use it and see the class at the same time? Perhaps you need an extension lead/adaptor/amplifier). With help the children will improve in their care, use and organization of equipment including art and craft materials. Finally, are the children wearing suitable clothing for dramatic work?

# Chapter 3: Primitive and Child Drama

There are elements in the drama of primitive peoples and in mythology, that provide a rich source of inspiration for child drama, meet children's needs and match their experience. This chapter is intended as an introduction to this material and it is hoped that from it teachers will select ideas and themes to initiate and develop improvisation and playmaking with their classes and be encouraged to study the subject further. The word 'primitive' is sometimes used in the derogatory sense. In this study of the nature and purpose of drama however it is used in the sense of 'non-derivative', that is, original, springing directly from the life-needs of a group of people.

Although the experiences of primitive man and those of children are of course separate (children are soon influenced by 'civilization'), there are some interesting parallels, as to some extent children pass through stages from primitive to 'civilized' as they develop. Also, even when we have reached maturity, our primitive heritage is still with us. Ideas and patterns in our minds for drama are passed on from generation to generation and have compelling force and vitality in educational use. Instinctive behaviour, spontaneity, direct responses to stimuli, contact with and exploration of, the environment come at the first stages.

Two significant features of primitive drama have been observed among many groups. First, the whole community takes part in some way, even though the most active part may be taken by only a section of people. All present give themselves and their attention wholeheartedly to the activity, to the focus, apparently deriving enjoyment, stimulus and energy by participating.

Drama, by its nature, demands participation and involvement and the enjoyment and benefit thereby derived is obvious to the teacher. Although we cannot expect full participation from all the children all the time, ways can be found of helping the reluctant or disabled child to experience this. Perhaps he can contribute a piece of art, or craft, written work, or sound accompaniment.

The second feature common to the drama of early peoples is the integration of that drama with many other art forms. In 'primitive' life, singing, speaking, shouting, dancing, acrobatic feats, playing instruments, body decoration, mock use of weapons, may all contribute to one event. Perhaps these various activities might be taking place at once, or in linked succession. Narrative and song is frequently interspersed with mimetic action. As the idea of art for art's sake developed with civilization, the arts became separated and the divisions between subjects, which many teachers now feel have become too distinct, occurred. At Primary School level, as the Plowden Report has emphasized, subject grouping and integrated work are considered desirable. In primitive life, this integrated event seems to fulfil a basic need, that of man's attempt to come to terms with his environment especially through group activities. The group expression emphasizes the cohesion and unity needed for survival, overriding personal considerations. Truly individual expression comes at a later stage.

Child play and also early dramatic expression is often an expression of coming to terms with life and environment. This can be seen in primitive drama too. Since man's first need is for food, the purpose of early dance dramas or ritual dramas is to secure a successful hunt or adequate crops. By the movement and vocal expression it is hoped that a good relationship with the forces of nature or spirits, gods or the unknown will be maintained or improved. Abstractions of the forces of nature may be represented: the river, fertility, the thunder. Sometimes the dance drama rehearses emotions, as in the war dance, and takes place before the event, as, for example, with the Masai people, before a lion hunt. Here the enactment is intended to increase strength and courage and to induce success by pre-doing. At other times the enactment takes place after the event, perhaps a straightforward imitation of animals or people, usually to celebrate and re-live the success and the hunt. An example is that of the Eskimo duck dance which after the hunt imitates the duck and its killing.

Imitation is a necessary feature of child and primitive life and learning. In primitive expression we may see the leader imitated; all chant or clap when he does. Or we may see an animal imitated, perhaps in order to gain power over it, or, in the case of totem tribes, in order to become one with the animal and thus promote its strength. Imitation is needed to achieve that secure state of doing, doing the same; an important feature of both primitive and early child drama. Imitation is attempted through movement, sound and body decoration or dressing up. It can have a comic effect, for example when the person being imitated is in ignorance of the fact – a popular occurrence in children's humour.

We can also see in both primitive and child drama energetic action, emotional release and expression such as fear, anger, gratitude, love, wonder, pity, exhilaration, despondency and disgust. It is beyond the scope of this book to give examples of all these, but the following extract from Tschiffely's *This Way Southward*,[1] describing the ritual feast of gratitude known as Camaruco, is interesting. This was held annually by South American Indians in honour of the great spirit who assisted their forefathers when they roamed over vast pampas and through the desert in pursuit of guanacos (ostrich) and other prey with which he rewarded good hunters.

> From different directions, Indians ride to a place previously agreed upon. Having tethered or hobbled their horses, they sit down, forming a vast circle, an opening being left towards the east. The men form the front row, the women sit behind, and the chiefs take their place in the middle. For some time nothing happens; but presently a number of men mount their horses and several times slowly ride round the circle of people. Then suddenly they dash off, hell for leather, towards the east where, sand and dust flying, the horses are brought to an abrupt standstill. One man then slowly rides on, still towards the east, acting as if he were about to meet someone. After a while he stops, and having gone through the motions of humbly greeting an invisible person, he turns his horse round, and acting as if he were leading someone by the hand, very slowly approaches the group of mounted men who make a gangway through which the chief actor rides. At this point the whole assembly – up to now seated in a circle – rises to its feet. The chief actor, followed by the other riders very slowly approaches the opening in the circle, and rides in alone, still going through the motions of leading a very tall person or rider by the hand. The chief, who is in charge of the ceremony, now steps forward to greet the invisible visitor, who is supposed to be none other than Futa Untru, the great spirit of the pampas (futa—great; untru—man or spirit).
>
> Now all the riders race round the outside of the circle, and everybody joins in their cries with yells of joy. This commotion lasts until a white horse is brought into the circle. Once its fore and hind legs have been tied together and it is otherwise held with lassos to make much movement impossible, the principal chief plunges a long knife into the unfortunate animal's heart, and

when it has been cut out of the body, an operation done with speed and dexterity, the Chief slowly walks round the circle of sitting people and sprinkles drops of blood over them.

After this everybody makes merry whilst the victim of the ceremony is cut up to be roasted over a number of fires. Other food and often much alcohol is consumed.

Revelry, gaiety, enjoyment, are important elements in dramatic expression which may also provide opportunity for weapon or mood practice, in primitive life, as in the following episode from the Noga tribes in north east India. It is described by Havemeyer in *The Drama of Savage Peoples.*[2]

> It (the dance drama) commences with a review of the warriors who later advance and retreat, parrying blows, and throwing spears as though in a real fight. They creep along in battle array, keeping as near the ground as possible so that nothing shows but a line of shields. When they are near enough to the imaginary enemy they spring up and attack. After they have killed the opposing party they grab tufts of grass, which represent the heads, and these they sever with their battle axes. Returning home they carry the clods over their shoulders as they would the heads of real men. At the village they are met by the women who join in a triumphant song and dance.

Here too we see the make-believe use of objects so common in child play.

Comedy is another important element. A particular sense of humour tends to belong to a particular culture – through the environment and needs of the people some things may be found relatively funny, holy, interesting, unusual, and so on. However, it is possible to offer as a broad generalization that both primitive peoples and children appear to respond with laughter in situations involving the misfortunes of others, as for example in the Phillipine Islands folk play where a traveller finds a beehive and is attacked by the bees. In many children's games we see this trait also, and even games to induce misfortune or inflict pain for the amusement of the onlookers or those in the know. Booby traps, self-incrimination traps, jeers, tricks and practical jokes come into this area of experience. Laughter is often induced by show of incorrect behaviour or speech, ignorance, foreigners, minority opinion, burlesque, slap-stick, parody. Surprises, transformation, incongruous size-relationships such as small men in large boots can also cause laughter reactions, and puns, riddles, topical jokes, rhymes or nonsense rhymes especially with children.

Character, situation and action including struggle or conflict are essential to Drama. How soon do specific characters emerge in early drama? The hero is perhaps the first to be noticed. Most authorities agree that one origin of the hero figure lies in ritual – the central figure of ritual – but as mythology developed from ritual the deeds of the central figure became important. Sympathy moved from the act of sacrifice to the victim, leading to the heroic myth. Here again, heroic characteristics vary from culture to culture; ethnological knowledge is required for explanations. It is possible to enumerate several kinds of hero generally popular; the hero who does brave deeds overcomes difficulties and conquers enemies by force of strength; the hero who finds answers and achieves success by his wit, sometimes he is a clever trickster, almost a villain. (For example, see descriptions of the cunning heroes favoured by the Wolof in Africa.[3]) Another kind of hero is the one who rises to heroic status from an unpromising start. He may be derided or persecuted by rivals or jealous bystanders; he may appear a simpleton or fool, but always achieves a brilliant, if unexpected triumph. Sometimes the hero is an animal or even an inanimate object, e.g. the gingerbread boy, or potato man of children's literature, or the coyote hero of Western plains Indians, or the spider hero of Eastern plains Indians. The scapegoat or martyr-hero are other manifestations, and as far as drama in the junior school is concerned, make their appearance in stories of religion and history. Often the death of the martyr hero is caused by treachery and his triumph is usually in death. An additional feature in heroic tales may be that of over action of the dominant heroic trait, leading to 'hubris' (see Greek mythology and drama) or pride. The true hero of course is made aware of this and eventually overcomes it.

However, one character does not usually make a drama although his inner conflict may do so. An opposing force or character is needed, often in the form of ogres or demons in primitive stories and folklore.[4, 5] Contrasting with heroes, they represent the dark, the inexplicable evil. There are trolls, gnomes, bogles, cyclops, djinns, kobolds, hobgoblins, monsters, bargeists, windigows, poltergeists, werewolves, necrophagous ghouls, wizards, awl-elbowed witches, dopple gangers and unnatural animals. When hero and ogre meet a fight often ensues. During the fight, physical prowess, acrobatics, feats of daring and courage are important and popular ingredients.

The theme of the journey is common in folklore, and indeed of psychological significance. In a simple way both hero and journey theme is seen in the 'follow-my-leader' game. In selecting journey themes for drama work, make use of this game idea and choose journeys that involve going into strange imaginary areas, on to unusual terrain such as underground (as Odysseus, Orpheus), into water (as Beowulf, Jonah), or into the desert or jungle, or up mountains (many heroes). Often there are extremes of weather conditions to contend with. There is always a reason for the journey – and again this must be borne in mind in drama lessons. Perhaps hunting, hiding, escaping, chasing, exploring, or discovering may be the reasons. In primitive drama an historically true journey may be enacted, from the remote or recent past history of the tribe, ranging from the simplest life scenes of fishing trips, to longer trading journeys. An example from the Euahlayi tribe of Australia, tells of the coming of the first boat up the Barwen. A log is hollowed out, plastered with mud, and painted to represent the boat. A smaller log is hollowed out and suitably placed to represent the funnel. First the natives pretend to be birds, and make bird noises when they see the boat. A group of armed natives approach fearfully. They confer together and discuss how to deal with this strange 'monster'. Tentatively they approach the river bank, but on board ship the fire is stoked and smoke emerges from the funnel; the natives are terrified. This idea of enacting an event from life can be a good theme for drama lessons.

The important dramatic elements of suspense and surprise are clearly present in the above example, and of course no drama is complete without them. Children like these elements too and once again we should make extended conscious use of what they already enjoy. The popular incident of a mistake can also contain the elements of surprise and suspense, for instance, in the Dyak native play:

A warrior is busy picking a thorn out of his foot, but is on the alert for the lurking enemy, with his weapons ready at hand. This enemy is suddenly discovered, and after some rapid attack and defence, a sudden lunge is made at him and he is dead on the ground. The taking of his head follows in pantomime. The story then concludes with the startling discovery that the slain is not an enemy at all but the brother of the warrior who has slain him. Then a magic-doctor charms life back into the man.

In both primitive and child mind, there is a strong feeling for magic, omens and the forces of nature, with no sharp divisions between man and nature or between present and future. Inanimate objects may come to life at any moment, they may be menacing and must be pacified or influenced. Shadows are sometimes associated with the supernatural. Some primitive men regard their shadows as vital parts of themselves and as such need protection. If his shadow is stamped on he may feel the injury as if it were done to him. Games with shadows are popular with children, both their own full-length shadows, and shapes they make with their hands. Magic and themes of wishes, dreams and transformation are rich in possibilities for drama, and frequently found in folklore. A popular transformation theme is that of birds changing into humans, for instance, in the Eskimo legend of the owl or in the Russian legend of the swan. This transformation theme is also seen in The Frog Prince story, and the Little Mermaid story of Hans Andersen. Every-day objects can alter or become animate, the environment can change in surprising ways in dream fantasies; colours, textures, shapes can alter, speeds can vary in odd ways – growing slower and slower or faster and faster – less or more erratic. Tension in the body can change – weightlessness can take over, or ways of travelling can change such as the use of arms or torso in place of legs.

Funeral games and ceremonies of death are a feature of both child and primitive life, also, as in the Dyak example quoted above, themes of healing and resurrection. The latter are seen in Spring rituals of rebirth and in children's games, in folk plays of many parts of the world, as well as in early English folk drama. An example of these is the Mummers play of St. George and the Dragon, where the doctor applies varied medicaments to infuse life into the main character.

In addition to drama themes from 'primitive' man, the form and manner of their enactment are worth considering in relation to class movement and speech work. In primitive life many of the various enactments follow a definite seasonal pattern, as also do many children's games. There is a useful source of material here for the teacher in customs of seasons, months, even days of the year, again soundly based in child-primitive needs at the root of cultural expression. Both in children's play and in 'primitive' dance drama, certain forms, floor patterns and activities prevail to a greater or lesser extent in many parts of the world. The teacher should be aware of these various elements and notice when they appear in children's work, and introduce them as part of his stimuli and content for child drama.

The circle, with its common-to-all focus and secure equality of position is as prevalent in folk or primitive dance and life as it is in children's games. Giving rise to continuous movement, this formation can be protective or menacing in expression. Sometimes there is an object or person around which one goes. Taking turns at entering the circle for solo or duo combat incidents also occurs as well as weaving patterns around an outside standing circle with or without linking hands to form a trellis of bridges. Sometimes a double circle is seen; one inside the other. Breaking the circle gives rise to a line with leader and followers, creating a different formation, seen in all processions. Two parallel lines approaching and retreating from one another is another feature of folk dance-drama and children's games, sometimes with an imaginary boundary placed between, sometimes including changes of place. Considerable use of energy, precision, ingenuity and rhythm is seen in the movement. Simple earth-bound steps and stamps contrast with jumping, whirling and acrobatic feats.

These early dramas may appear earthbound, and may refer symbolically to the earth itself, earth the life-giver, brutal mysterious, solid, dark and fertile; the place of hell, yet the birthplace of vitality. However, they may also refer to the other elements in some magico-religious way; to the air spirits with awareness of omens, wind, witches, birds; or to water with its contrasts of calm and raging, advance and retreat – the unfettered shapelessness of water, the mirage in the desert. Ritual ceremonies take place in honour of the spirits of these elements, also of fire, with its vibrant destructive qualities.

Rhythm is an important element in drama: the rhythm of preparation, action and recovery, of attention, intention, decision, of anticipation and the event, of meeting and parting, or character rhythms of different personalities. Both movement and speech uses contrasts between breath-based rhythmic phrases and heartbeat-pulse-based rhythmic phrases and also the effects of rallentando and accelerando. All these can be applied directly to the drama lesson, both in conceiving an overall rhythmic structure for the lesson, and in providing rhythmic stimulus and training. Drama lessons are more satisfying when rhythm is developed. Too often the 'primitive' physical nature of rhythm is forgotten and it is taught artificially as a musical or metric structure to be tapped or counted out. However, sometimes accurately stressed metric rhythms are needed, as in machine scenes, possibly with disciplined increase and decrease of speed; at other times a non-metric rhythm will be more appropriate – as in sequences of human responses and activities arising from them. Also, change of attention develops its own free rhythm creating interesting patterns for both individuals and groups. Part of the child's enjoyment of nonsense syllables lies in their rhythm, and an awareness of both natural and stylized speech rhythms can be developed. There is use of meaningless or nonsense syllables, in primitive song or chant, most obvious in the refrain, but also as almost complete verses. For instance, this Objibwa song in which the only word is the first one, meaning the 'bravest man':

Ungitched-ah, hey ah heyah
Hey ah heyah ah ah heyah heyahah
Hey ah heyah hey ah heyah heyah heyah heyahhey.[6]

Unlike our fa la la la's, when used in this way syllables may be the remains of obsolete words.

The use of repetition is an important aspect of rhythm, rhythmic development and variation. Repetitive patterns are prominent in child and primitive origins of language.

There are several kinds of repetition that can be made use of in classroom work. There is narrative repetition in which part or all of the story is repeated, rhythmic repetition as in songs, and incremental repetition as in folk ballads when stanzas are partially repeated.

There is also accumulative repetition of which a recent pop song makes successful use:

lines 1 I
+ echo chorus
2 I want
+ echo chorus
3 Oh I want you
+ echo chorus
4 I want you to be
+ echo chorus
5 I want you to be my baby.
+ echo chorus
+ echo refrain

lines 1 Will
2 Will you
3 Will you please
4 Will you please tell
5 Will you please tell me yes.

The following is a child's example:

The old ebony box
The old old ebony box
The old old old ebony ebony box
The old old old old ebony ebony ebony box box.

Sequential repetition is the name given to repetition of the kind used in 'The House that Jack Built', moving the action forward. Spiral repetition will be familiar to teachers of infant age range in stories or rhymes which carry action upwards – 'the tree was on the hill, the bough was on the tree, the twig was on the bough, the leaf was on the twig,' etc. In anaphonic repetition the beginning words of a phrase are repeated in the next, and in litany repetition the refrain device is used to make an ABCBDB, etc., form.

Repetition on a larger scale takes place in parallelism, when a mirror effect is achieved by having a reverse echo of part one in part two. (Literary examples can be found especially in Anglo Saxon and Middle English verse.) A chain parallel is the term given to a form which links clauses, the end of one clause starting the next. For example:

That which the palmer worm hath left
Hath the locust eaten;
And that which the locust hath left
Hath the canker worm eaten.

Sounds are sometimes repeated in order to achieve increase of speed, and tension leading to climax, as in the following Australian aborigines kangaroo tracking description:

I bin gooooooo I bin go I bin go I bin go
I bin go I bin go I bin go
I bingoIbingoIbingo
I bin sneakin I bin sneakin
I bin sneakin I bin follerin im

I bin follerin im
Follerim follerim follerim CRACK!
Capped im dis time by Chrise
Proper good one
No more gammon![6]

Enjoyment of ritual pattern and repetition of all kinds is obvious in children's play and in folk tales – for instance in the Zuni myth, where forty people enter one after the other and the same story is repeated to each, or the Chinook Indian tales where often five brothers have the same adventure, the first four perish, the youngest is successful.

The use of repetition and its development by the teacher with the children can assist confident use of language and vocabulary. For instance in a simple way during the drama the teacher as narrator can launch a descriptive phrase and the children restate all or part of it to make an echo. At a later stage they will be able to repeat it but add to the adjectives, to help to build up a climax. For instance, during a fantasy play attempted with nine year olds the following simple exchange took place during improvisations:

*Teacher:* The storm clouds gather overhead, purple and black,
*Class:* The storm clouds gather overhead, purple and black,
*Teacher:* The storm clouds gather overhead, purple and black.
*Member of class:* The storm clouds gather overhead, large and dark.
*Teacher:* The large, dark storm clouds gather overhead,
*Class:* The large, dark storm clouds gather overhead.
*Member of class:* The large, dark storm clouds engulf us all!
*All:* Engulf us all!

This technique is especially appropriate for narrative laments or battle songs. (See its use in the Bible, e.g. Lamentations III 1–15.) Children also enjoy repetition in the form of assonance and alliteration.

Question and answer form is an important one in relation to drama. We can see it operating in Greek tragedy and in early medieval liturgical drama. Again, repetition is often included as in this extract from a Pygmy lament for the dead:

Q. The animal runs, it passes, it dies.
    And it is the great cold.
A. It is the great cold of the night, it is the dark.

Q. The bird flies, it passes, it dies.
And it is the great cold.
A. It is the great cold of the night, it is the dark.
Q. The fish flies, it passes, it dies.
And it is the great cold.
A. Man eats and sleeps. He dies.
And it is the great cold.[7]

And from the popular chants of children:

S: You remind me of a man.
Q: What man?
S: A man of power.
Q: What power?
S: The power of hoodoo.
Q: Who do?
S: You do.
Q: What?
S: Remind me of a man, etc. etc.

A linguistic use of the circle form described earlier.

Onomatopoeia is popular in primitive and child language. Some attractive examples from Coeur d'Alene Indians include

| | |
|---|---|
| opam pam | for the noise of the bow |
| xuts xuts xuts | for bones breaking |
| ludidi ludidi | for spiders spinning |
| otsaxsax | for grinding teeth |
| alilili | for the feel of cold water |

Obviously these examples can only be fully effective if appropriate use is made of rhythm and vowel sound.

Finally, a comment on the beginnings and endings. As they become interested in and ready for conscious use and manipulation of structure in playmaking, children can be encouraged to invent lively, appropriate beginnings and endings, which they usually find more difficult. This should not be forced in the early stages when either the work will be 'open-ended' or the security of a familiar equivalent to 'Once upon a time' and 'lived happily ever after' is likely to be chosen. Formalized beginnings and endings are popular with children and are also seen in 'primitive' stories and dramas. An example comes from the Bahamas at the end of the last century where every story began with 'Once it was a time', and ended with 'E bo ban, my story's en'. Sometimes the group joins in as when the Hausa story teller announces 'gatanan, Gatanan' (a story, a story), and the response comes 'Ta ja, ta ko mo' (let it go, let it come).

BOOK REFERENCES

1. A. F. Tschiffely, *This Way Southward*, Heinemann
2. L. Havemeyer, *The Drama of Savage Peoples*, Yale University Press 1916.
3. Geoffrey Gorer, *Africa Dances*, W. W. Norton & Co.
4. Robin Palmer, *Dragons, Unicorns and Other Magical Beasts*, Hamish Hamilton
5. Peter Lunn, *Fabulous Beasts*, Thames and Hudson
6. John Greenaway, *Literature among the Primitives*, Folklore Association
7. C. M. Bowra, *Primitive Song*, Weidenfeld and Nicolson

**See also**

J. H. M. Beattie, 'Social Anthropology' (in *The New Outline of Modern Knowledge*, ed. Pryce-Jones).
Ruth Benedict, *Patterns of Culture*, Routledge and Kegan Paul.
F. Boas (ed.), *The Function of Dance in Human Society*, N.Y.
Peter Brook, *The Empty Space*, MacGibbon and Kee.
Thomas Bullfinch, *The Age of Fable*, Fawcett Publications.
Elizabeth Cook, *The Ordinary and the Fabulous*, C.U.P.
Frieda Fordham, *An Introduction to Jung's Psychology*, Penguin Books.
Frankfort, Wilson, and Jacobson, *Before Philosophy*, Penguin Books.
J. G. Frazer, *The Golden Bough*, Macmillan.
Alice Gomme, *The Traditional Games of England, Scotland and Ireland*, Dover.
Jane Harrison, *Prolegomena to the Study of Greek Religion*, Meridian Books.
W. Carew Hazlitt, *Faiths and Folklore of the British Isles*, Blom.
E. O. James, *Myth and Ritual in the Ancient Near East*, Thames and Hudson.
E. O. James, *Seasonal Feasts and Festivals*, Thames and Hudson.
Carl Jung (ed.), *Myth and Symbol*, Aldus.
Lucy Mair, *Primitive Government*, Penguin Books.
Margaret Mead, *Coming of Age in Samoa*, Penguin Books.
John Middleton (ed.), *Myth and Cosmos*, Natural History Press.
Iona and Peter Opie, *The Lore and Language of Schoolchildren*, Oxford.
Iona and Peter Opie, *Children's Games in Street and Playground*, Oxford.
William Ridgeway, *The Dances and Dramatic Dances of the Non-European Races*.
Curt Sachs, *World History of the Dance*, W. W. Norton.
Kay Birket-Smith, *Primitive Man and his Ways*, Odhams.
Lewis Spence, *The Outlines of Mythology*, Premier.
Joan la Fontaine (ed.), *On the Interpretation of Ritual*, Barnes and Noble.
Elizabeth Thomas, *The Harmless People*, Knopf.

# Chapter 4: The First Stage

*'Would you tell me/please/which way I ought to go from here?'*
*'That depends a good deal on where you want to get to/' said the Cat.*
Lewis Carroll, *Alice in Wonderland*

The younger child is being the thing or person he represents, he is not consciously pretending. The 'Let's play school/house . . . Let's pretend . . .', comes at a later stage. In drama activity he is interested in re-living and imitating events of his home and near neighbourhood. The real world and things he has seen in it can and do reappear in his dramatic play: his mother and father at work in the house, local characters such as the bus driver, the postman, the coalman, the policeman, the petrol attendant, the dustman, a shopkeeper. Other more generalized characters also appear. These are likely to include a train driver, fireman, an air pilot, a captain of a ship and TV characters according to the child's experience. Local journeys and the doings and simple adventures of these characters provide plenty of ideas for drama content. For town children, the life and objects of the street can be used in a real or fantasy way: cars, buses, pillar boxes, drain covers, manholes, telephone kiosks, telegraph poles, lamp posts, kerbs, railings, zebra crossings, shop windows. For country children the visits of delivery vans, the vet and occupations concerning animals, crops, market, streams or ditches are more appropriate. Stories and poems about these various interests can be found in most Junior libraries and Infant Schools, and provide good ancillary reading and listening material.

In work on some of these ideas, drama will be part of the general activity in the classroom. For instance, focusing on the work of the postman and the local post office is likely to include making a class post office and uniforms with drama arising from counter clerks' and customers' dealings and conversations. A postman can be invited to visit the classroom, and the children be given opportunity to ask questions. Things to do in connection with this might include:

a visit to the local sorting office

use of a demonstration phone from the G.P.O. (or from a junk shop)

use of stamps, coins and weights

finding and using information concerning addressing/sending a letter, stamps, postmarks, times of collection, times of delivery, the journey the letter makes

make a simple map of the postman's round (either to include own house or school area).

Teacher and children can collect news cuttings, stamps, postmarks, pictures and posters for classroom display, and write and post letters to each other and other classes in the class post box.

Seasonal characteristics and activities provide further appropriate material for drama in the Infant School, also other aspects of nature such as the sun, moon and stars, trees and clouds, water and fire; insects, birds, animals. In fact, throughout the Infant School day opportunities for developing drama occur, especially during creative activities and story time.

Stories and magic that seem to take the child away from the everyday world are indeed part of drama play. However, a young child does not register the sharp division between animate and inanimate, reality and fantasy, truth and magic that exists for adults.

A simple beginning with the reception class is made with stories and drama in finger play.

e.g. Here is the beehive
Where are the bees?
Hidden away where nobody sees.
Soon they come creeping out of the hive
1.., 2.., 3.., 4.., 5!

or Ten little soldiers standing in a row,
They all bow down to the captain low
They march to the left, they march to the right,
They all stand straight, ready to fight.
Along comes a man with a great big gun
And you ought to see those soldiers run, and run!

and in contrasting mood:

Here are Grandma's spectacles
Here is Grandma's cap
And this is the way she folds her hands
And lays them in her lap.

The approach with infants should always be friendly, informal and imaginative, encouraging and developing speech, movement, ideas and work with others. Attempts should not be interrupted for correction or creativity and spontaneity goes. Also, the teacher should avoid having pre-conceived ideas of a finished product and resist the temptation of 'improving' the child's work.

## Drama from sounds

The teacher can begin by playing a percussion instrument or by making a simple sound such as tapping a table top in a definite way and asking, 'What does this make you think of?' Answers might include 'A thick forest', 'a giant', 'a soldier'. Then the teacher (as he develops his rhythm, still keeping it simple) 'What is he doing/what is happening?' Answers such as 'Climbing a tree', 'climbing a tower', 'riding a horse'. Teacher: 'Listen again. This is what he saw/what came along next' (plays a contrasting sound); 'What is it?' Answers might be 'A spider', 'an ant', 'a mouse', etc. (and be prepared for, welcome, encourage and use any unexpected suggestions here, such as 'an Eskimo', 'a red umbrella', 'a football team manager'). Teacher: 'And here is what happened when he saw the. . . .' (makes another sound). Answers, perhaps, 'He chased the mouse!', 'he jumped off his horse', 'he picked up the umbrella and a high wind blew and took him up into the sky!' Then try it all through again giving more opportunity for movement and speech, everybody being everything as mentioned.

I would suggest that three, or for older children four, contrasting sounds are sufficient in one 'story'. These few are then easily recognizable when they are repeated, and the children will respond to them with confidence. Instructions should not be given as to exactly how the sounds should be used, but the children should react as they wish and be given the chance to try and try again. They are happy and able to change characters quickly: they can be the forest and the spider; or even two at once: the knight and his horse. Incidentally, the logical sequence that older children expect is not a necessity to the young child. We can see this sometimes when a child is playing alone with toys: orders are not necessarily given in a logically connected sequence.

After providing the initial stimulus or simply opportunity for Drama, the teacher's help and care is required in extending and developing the work, both in movement and speech. He can also work to improve his own improvisation, story-telling and percussion playing. In percussion playing or making the sounds, vary the qualities, speeds, and climax size and placing in the phrase. The movement towards and away from the climax needs careful shaping. Also make use of regular and irregular rhythms using metric and non-metric pulse appropriately. Timing is all-important: allow an adequate length of time for action, thought and thorough movement – drama experience to take place. The sounds change when the mood, character, scene or situation changes and their use helps to strengthen and organize the drama. At first, as indicated above, the teacher makes the sound but gradually the children can join in and eventually take more of the initiative in both finding and using sounds. It is helpful if some of the instruments suitable to be used in this way can be suspended from a rack (e.g. an old wooden clothes horse). Sometimes story ideas such as the one above can be used for work with sound and drama, or alternatively work around a theme can be developed, such as 'The Jungle'. Here sound, movement, art and craft could link together with drama experience to make a piece of integrated work. Sometimes the children's own painting can initiate a theme or story-play with sound effects and accompaniment.

In integrated work the teacher needs to decide where the emphasis is to be. This applies especially to the movement content. Movement in drama is naturally of an imitative kind and imaginative associations are encouraged. Sometimes when young children are absorbed in an imaginative idea they lose the movement experience. Therefore the teachers should watch for this and also provide opportunity for movement experience (leading later to dance) where movement possibilities are explored for their own sake, without a dramatic stimulus. For specific advice on movement at all stages in the Primary School, see the book list at the end of this chapter[1–6].

## Story-playing, dramatization, playmaking

All the drama work discussed here is intended to be improvised with and by the children. This is the suggested way of working whether the stories are originally told or read by the teacher or made up with the children as in the example stimulated by sound above, or in the Ideas Game well documented in Peter Slade's *Child Drama*[7]. The latter method is a good way of starting as it is likely to ensure the absorption and lively, creative spontaneity and sense of achievement which should, we hope, come from drama experience! Before selecting story, themes or characters for drama work, consult Chapters 1 and 2 where specific fundamental story ideas are mentioned.

The story or idea needs to be well told or presented, simply, directly and with vitality yet avoiding the pitfalls of over-dramatic delivery. The aim when action begins is to develop the story-playing beyond an exercise of memory to a real drama and creative experience. This is again where the teacher's assistance is essential. Questions asked by the teacher help children to extend their thinking and movement and speech expression. Remember, speech should flow from activity and from having something to communicate. Much drama development can occur through discussion with the class. However, remember what drama is doing: do not allow too much talking to take place before action begins. As with drama at any age, there must be opportunity for individual and group work, with conflict, action, situation, climax, atmosphere and characterization. With infants, the conflict needs to be of circumstance rather than character, since their main interest is in the action. For instance, the forest has grown up round the enchanted castle, so we all hack it down. It is not necessary to pay attention to detail as long as the action is kept going. As playmaking develops, the sense of continuity through the action, with dramatic climax, rather than a collection of episodes, should emerge. Each happening constitutes a small scene and should introduce a new person, a new turn of events, or a different mood and climax.

## Dressing-up box

Clothes and materials for dressing-up are a known source of delight to the young child and should be included in the equipment of every classroom. The items for children's use should be purposefully chosen and frequently renewed.

## Puppets

The making and use of puppets should be included in Infants' and Juniors' drama experience. See Chapter 6 for suggestions.

## Playmaking from a nursery rhyme

There was an old woman tossed up in a basket,
Seventeen times as high as the moon.
Where was she going, I couldn't but ask it,
For in her hand she carried a broom.
'Old woman, old woman, old woman', quoth I,
'Where are you going to, up so high?'
'To brush the cobwebs off the sky!'
'May I go with you?' 'Aye, bye and bye!'

(from the *Oxford Book of Nursery Rhymes*[8])

To encourage improvised drama and playmaking from a rhyme such as this, questions such as the following should be asked, and some of the answers briefly discussed with the children.

'Where was the old woman going?'
'Why was she going there?'
'Why did she have to go?'
'Where did she come from?'
'What was her house like?'
'What was near her house?'
'Who asked/told her to go?'
'How did she get the basket?'
'Was it specially made – who made it?'
'Did anyone see her get into the basket and take off?'
'Did she ever get there?'
'What happened when she got there?'
'Did she come back for you?'
'Where did you go?'

From the answers given it is usually possible to stimulate lively and interesting dramatic activity. Perhaps the King has asked her to go, perhaps there is a national cobweb collecting competition in progress, perhaps she is a strange old witch. Group scenes could occur in the palace, in the market place making the basket, seeing the old woman off (all blowing up her balloon) and if she visits other places, groups can provide the inmates. It is an appealing rhyme and implies interesting happenings, notably the journey which is such a fundamentally satisfying theme and one in which the young child's growing movement ability can be fully used.

## Playmaking from a story

*'Sound the alarm! or how the city got its new gates'*

The structure of this story-play is a suitable one for beginners being based on 'a day in the life of . . .'. We are asleep, we wake up and the day begins; activities increase. A crisis/practical problem occurs: it is overcome in a practical way. The end of the day: sleep. The teacher acts as narrator perhaps as italicised, allowing time for action, sound accompaniment and speech arising both from the story and from children's suggestions

*We are in a city in a country far away. It is early morning. First we hear the sounds of the city waking up and the day begins.*/Clang of metal on metal as the sentries of the morning watch turn and salute, their spears knocking against their shields; the dry clatter of donkeys' hooves on their way to the bazaar; the gossiping of women round the well; the swish of brush and water as the royal sweepers clean the palace steps and alleyways. For this is the city of a great and princely Ruler; and the royal sweepers, who are always kept busy cleaning the palace are preparing for the weekly visit of the great Ruler to the market.

*In the market workers are setting up their booths and starting their work.*/ The jewellers make intricate ornaments from silver and coral, pearls, rubies and twisted golden wire. The shoemakers tap and stretch the fine leather; they make shoes as bright as glass, as light as feathers, as strong as steel. They nail gold heels to scarlet slippers fit for princesses and they make long purple boots for the palace horsemen. In the sweetmakers' booths the dough is frying, sugar is crackling, honey is bubbling. The workers here are kept hot and busy tending the fires, stirring the pots, rolling the dough, carrying the vats of boiling syrup. The embroiderers work quietly at their trade. They handle lengths of heavy cloth and trace twisting patterns in brightly coloured silks. They untangle and wind the threads, they shake out any creases in the delicate fabrics and hang them out, shining in the morning sun.

*And now the merchants come.*/*And now*/'Cymbals, sound!' *The great Ruler himself, with his purse bearers and body-guards.*/He is at the sweet stall, just about to pop a sugar plum into the royal mouth, when *drums* are heard and the alarm signal! *The enemy has attacked*!/The merchants and workers hastily pack up their wares and hide. Some stay cowering behind the booths, others go scuttling up nearby alleyways, clutching their possessions to them. Others know of secret cellars, and make straight for these. Alas, the enemy has stormed the gates, the gates are broken, *the great Ruler* himself is surrounded; he *is captured and taken away/.*

Just as the merchants and workers are climbing out of their hiding places, *messengers arrive/*asking for ransom. The merchants set up a howl of dismay, but they count out the money. *The great Ruler is welcomed back into the city./*He makes sure that *new gates are made, very very much stronger than the old ones./*Although it is very hot, everyone works on making the gates until the end of the day. *Then, tired and weary, they all pack up/*their belongings.

The sounds of the day grow fainter: the dry clatter of donkeys hooves on their way back from the bazaar; the clang of metal on metal as the sentries of the evening watch turn and salute; the women's gossip as they leave the well and the swish of brush and water as the royal sweepers clean the palace steps for the last time that day. *Finally, everyone reaches home and falls asleep./*

In the Junior School, the hall should be made available for Drama activity. When this is done, the work should begin with movement or movement and sound. Every member of the class should be working at the same time, freely moving about the space. (Consult pp. 29–30, 37, 46, 99–103 for further suggestions, also the book list at the end of this chapter.)

In this story-play there are opportunities for experience in contrasts of movement and mood, in the use of simple pathways, in legitimate fighting (as suggested in Chapter 5) and sound accompaniment. As with any tale, the teacher can select as much or as little of it to be used as a basis for drama as he or the children wish, remembering that even if the continuity of the whole story is wanted, anything unsuitable for class action can be narrated. (The basis of this story are from *Cymbals Sound for the King* by Enid Barr[9]). Also well suited for this treatment and age group are *The Giants, The Lazy Tribe* or *The Mountain* in *Infant Drama* by Ronald James.[10]

## Playmaking for mid-top Infants and for Lower Juniors

An adaptation of the story 'The Magic Pot' provides a good example of the kind of story to use with this age group. It has a well defined, easily understood structure, it has humour, it has contrasting characters, and variety of group activity. It is a drama-story easy for the teachers to organize and develop unobtrusively by being the narrator. With older or more experienced classes one or more of the children could be the narrator. Or, of course, the narration can be omitted altogether.

Briefly, a drama version of the story could be this:

A man finds a dirty old pot in his yard. Much to his surprise it begins to speak: 'Clean me and polish me and put me on the fire!' The old man is mystified and takes the pot in to his old woman who decides of course the dirty pot must be cleaned. As soon as the pot has been cleaned it speaks again: 'I skip, I skip!' The old folk ask, 'Where do you skip?' The pot replies: 'I skip to the house of the Rich Man, where all his cooks are making puddings!'

And off goes the pot on his journey to the Rich Man's house. When he arrives there he makes his way to the kitchen and says: 'I'm cleaned and I'm polished and I want to be filled!' and because the Pot is Magic all the Rich Man's cooks put their puddings into the pot.

Back goes the pot to the Old Man and the Old Woman who are very pleased to see all the tasty puddings. After they have eaten as much as they are able and have put the rest in the larder, the Pot speaks again: 'Clean me and polish me and put me on the fire!' The Old Woman does so. Then: 'I skip, I skip!' 'Where do you skip?' 'I skip to the house of the Rich Man where he's picking his apples!' And off goes the pot on his journey to the Rich Man's house. When he arrives there he makes his way to the orchard and he says: 'I'm cleaned and I'm polished and I want to be filled!'

So all the Rich Man's apple pickers put their apples into the Pot. Back goes the Pot to the Old Man and the Old Woman, who are very pleased to see all the juicy fruit. After they have eaten as much as they can and stored the rest, the Pot speaks again: 'Clean me and polish me and put me on the fire!' The Old Woman does so. Then: 'I skip, I skip!' 'Where do you skip?' 'I skip to the house of the Rich Man, where he's counting his money!' And off goes the Pot again, on his journey to the Rich Man's house. When he arrives there he makes his way to the counting house where the Rich Man is himself and says: 'I'm cleaned and I'm polished and I want to be filled!'

So the Rich Man and all his servants in the counting house pour as many golden pieces into the pot as it can hold. When it is full, the Pot goes off again back to the Old Man and the Old Woman who are overjoyed to have the money.

The next day, the Pot says again: 'Clean me and polish me and put me on the fire!' The Old Woman does so, wondering where the Pot will be off to this time.

'I skip, I skip!'

'Where do you skip?'

'I skip. . . . . OVER THE HILLS AND FAR AWAY!' and off goes the Pot. When the old people see the Pot going away, they follow, but he goes too fast for them. The cooks and the apple pickers, the servants and the Rich Man himself all try to catch the Pot, but he goes too fast for them too. So they return home so tired that they fall asleep.

An alternative beginning is: 'An old man and his wife are so poor that all they have left is one cow.' The old man goes out to sell it. Leading the animal along the lane, he meets a man with a pot who suggests he makes an exchange with the cow. At first the old man is reluctant, but then the Pot speaks: 'Buy me! Buy me!' So although feeling rather awkward, the Old Man agrees to part with his cow. Afraid of what his wife might say he ties the Pot to the cow post in the byre for the night.

In the morning his wife is very upset, but she is just in the middle of scolding her husband when much to their surprise the Pot speaks: 'Wash me and scour me and put me on the fire!', etc. etc.

Also, any alternatives can be used for the Rich Man's servants' occupations. For instance, the Pot could visit the barns where corn is being shovelled and stored, or the cellar where wine is being stamped out of the grapes, etc. etc., according to the movement experience which the teacher feels his class would enjoy and benefit from.

A theme which can run through the play is that of the cruel Rich Man: he has caused the poverty of the old couple and at the end the Pot either goes after him and chases him away, or he is so annoyed with the Pot taking so much of his goods, that he grabs at the Pot and, getting hold of it, is lifted up into the air. The Pot flies away with the Rich Man who is never seen again. This ending is more interesting but more difficult for the children and teacher to organize.

The procedure with a story such as this is:

1. Tell the story, arousing interest and imagination.
2. (Preferably after some time has elapsed, e.g. the next day) in the

movement lesson introduce movements needed in the story (with opportunities in (a)-(c) and (e) for partner work for children ready for this), e.g. (a) busy pudding baking: the use of imaginary large sized basins which need several people to lift them and pour from them, carrying large boxes or bags of sugar and currants and tipping them into the pudding mixture; large scale stirring movements; stoking the oven; getting fuel for the oven; rolling out the pastry, etc.

(b) Climbing, stretching and picking fruit, carrying baskets, loading baskets

(c) Precise money counting, heaving sacks of gold along the ground; pouring coins into containers

(d) Washing, scrubbing, scouring, polishing a pot

(e) Pulling along an unwilling cow to market

(f) Being the Pot and going on journeys as the Pot

(g) Being the Rich Man

(h) Being the Old Man or Woman

3. Encourage the development of spontaneity.

The whole class should be given opportunity for movement experience as indicated above which can have appropriate sound accompaniment. Then, with teacher as narrator, the story can be acted, bringing more life and action to it than in the original story. The children can at first all be everything as mentioned (the teacher giving plenty of time for the movement to happen) and then if they are ready for this development, they can choose which group to be in. In the latter case the structure of a play will emerge, and the groups can be placed around the floor of the hall – cottage, kitchen, orchard, counting house – allowing for plenty of journey space between each group. Each time the Pot is filled, the servants concerned are in its power and realize too late what they have done – they can try to catch the Pot, but in vain and return to their work.

The Rich Man could come at the last moments of Pot filling and try to stop them and/or the Pot – also in vain. However, the final climax must be felt strongly so each time the servants and/or Rich Man could get nearer to catching the Pot. (If several children would like to be Pots, Rich Man, or Old Men/Women, there is no reason why they should not be.) Incidentally, the Pot(s) will have to be encouraged to take a circuitous route from cottage to Rich Man's house, rather than direct steps across the room. The children can be helped to follow the departure of the Pot into the air, focusing round the room and up and away until they imagine the Pot a dot in the distance. (If the teacher thinks the word 'skip' for the Pot's travelling might lead to stilted movement, of course he could change it to 'hop', 'run', or even 'hop-skip-jump' might be preferred.)

Children's own plays could evolve from discussion in answer to 'Where did the Pot come from?' 'Why?' 'When?' Also the children could speak during the action or make up words for the various scenes, e.g. dialogue between the Old Man and Woman, servants calling after the Pot or a chant for the counting house scene – 'We count the money, count the money, clinkety, clinkety, clink', was one refrain made up for a chant, with accompanying percussion noises of money clinking, by a group of seven-year-olds, when they worked on this play with me.

### A description of a class play which was based on a Spanish folktale (Lower-mid Juniors) 'The Devil and the Princesses'

This was acted out in groups on the floor of a hall:

Group one: The devil and his assistants
Group two: Courtiers and castle
Group three: The princesses
Group four: The knight and his companions
Group five: The local peasants

1. First we are in the devil's cave where his assistants are working as hard as they can but not hard enough to please the devil. He decides he needs women to work in his cave. He wants the best, so he sets out to capture the princesses who live in the nearby castle.
2. The devil bewitches the castle and captures the princesses. The castle falls in ruins and everyone flees.
3. A noble knight seeks adventure. He meets:
   Blowo who has great blowing power
   Porto who has superhuman strength for carrying things
   Ropo who has deft rope-making ability and
   Listeno who has specially acute sharpness of hearing.
   They approach the ruined, brambly, castle. A storm blows up (possibly this could be caused by the devil) but Blowo sends it away.

Porto goes ahead to force his way into the castle, but it is still bewitched. Listeno hears a cry from the well. Ropo gathers a group of local peasants together and with their help makes a rope.

4. The rope is let down over the side of the well and the knight descends into darkness. At the bottom of the well he finds a cave and all the princesses, chained to a rock who beg to be saved. The devil and his assistants spring out – there is a fight. The knight with his four men win and lead the princesses to safety.
5. The palace is rebuilt by the peasants, the palace people return and there is general rejoicing. The knight and his four friends shake hands over the well and go their different ways.

With older children more detailed discussion can take place in developing a story-play such as these. The teacher must accept suggestions from as many people as possible, quickly and tactfully selecting those that are suitable for immediate use. (Do not worry if there is little response at first. With encouragement it will grow.)

Character, setting and situation must always be made real to the children. Sometimes this can be achieved by drawing attention to similarities and differences between the story setting, characters and characters' feelings, and their own. In the case of a long journey it can be compared with their own journey to school. The children can discuss with the teacher which episodes and characters they wish to act and at which point their play should begin. With the older children too, far less structuring by the teacher is needed, and in the Junior school they are increasingly able to work on their own in groups, and with their own leaders. They outgrow the need for teacher as narrator and can cope with more detail in both action and characterization. A growing critical sense and sense of play structure leads them nearer to adult forms of drama, but their work should remain essentially child drama. We continue to encourage the attitudes to creative work established in the Infant School, the involvement, the absorption. Ted Hughes' advice to children when writing can be followed in drama activity: 'do one thing . . . imagine what you're writing about. See it and live it. Don't think it up laboriously, as if you were working out mental arithmetic. Just look at it, touch it, smell it, listen to it, turn yourself into it.'[11]

Themes for drama can still include everyday subjects, but with the older children it is generally easier to start with imaginative, mythological or historical themes. In playmaking initiated from stories, try to choose those with varied, fast moving plots. Younger Juniors enjoy wishes, riddles and far away places in their drama. Adventures remain popular at the Junior stage and can become more complicated, journeys over land, sea; through caves or air, are undertaken with alacrity. Themes should also include grotesque and comic elements. Chapter 2, 3, 5 and 6 should be consulted for other suggestions, themes and lesson content.

During their time in the Junior school, children will become ready to take on solo roles in drama. Here is a short, simple Chinese legend in which solo roles have importance.

## A jar full of ants

Briefly, the scenes could include:

1. Group scene: the news of the pot of gold being voiced in the market place. Rumours spreading
2. In twos or families; the news being brought home; reactions.
3. The class as individuals; the neighbour overhears and goes to find the pot.
4. Group scene: reactions of the family to the gold coming through the roof: perhaps bringing in the whole group for celebration as the family buy gifts for all.

Action could be attempted with the whole class, or several versions could be tried in groups, simultaneously, within the class. If one smaller group uses it, 1. could be omitted and 4. limited.

*The Story*

A man tells his wife that he has heard there is a pot of gold secretly hidden up on the mountainside, beneath a tree. He says that after he has had a good sleep he will fetch it. But a neighbour overhears this and hurries off to be the first to discover the gold. He finds the place and digs for a long time. He finds the pot but it only contains ants. He is very angry and goes to his neighbour's house, climbs on to the roof and tears some tiles away to make a hole. He aims the ants through the gap towards a hole in his neighbour's mosquito net. But gold falls out of the jar. The man on the roof looks again into the jar and finds one coin left – payment for his work.

In the early stages it is often helpful to provide a friend or servant for the solo character. Many of the stories which the children will want to act will contain a central solo figure, often in conflict with another solo figure, or with several in turn, eventually returning in triumph. This is a pattern which recurs in many heroic tales of a quest when several characters or strange creatures have to be met and overcome before the hero can return to claim his reward. At first have a group of heroes or choose stories with groups rather than solo characters in conflict. In any theme chosen, it is the underlying conflict and implications for the people involved that must be experienced; or a problem and how it is dealt with. Simply acting out a story is not drama experience. Also, we know that the age from approximately eight to twelve is the phase in which values are created, standards of work and lines of conduct are established. So an opportunity is missed if serious themes (including legends, stories, real life adventure, stories of men's achievements) are not investigated or are dismissed in a superficial way. The suggestions adults make are very important at this time. However the child should not be hurried or rushed into judgements. He likes to find his own explanation of the world, acceptable to himself.

BOOK REFERENCES

1. Rudolph Laban, *Modern Educational Dance*, Macdonald & Evans
2. Joan Russell, *Creative Dance in the Primary School*, Macdonald & Evans
3. Jean Carroll and Peter Lofthouse, *Creative Dance with Boys*, Macdonald & Evans
4. Valerie Preston, *A Handbook for Modern Educational Dance*, Macdonald & Evans
5. Marian North, *A Simple Guide to Movement Teaching*, Marian North
6. Diana Jordan, *Childhood and Movement*, Blackwell
7. Peter Slade, *Child Drama*, University of London Press
8. *The Oxford Book of Nursery Rhymes*, Oxford
9. Enid Barr, 'Cymbals Sound for the King', *From Story into Drama*, Heinemann
10. Ronald James, *Infant Drama*, Nelson
11. 'Capturing Animals', a broadcast to schools reprinted in *Listening and Writing*, B.B.C. Autumn 1961

**See also**

Peter Lofthouse, *Dance*, in this series

# Chapter 5: The Second Stage

## Drama from a beginning, a central section or an ending

After hearing the first part of a story, the children can be encouraged to invent their own endings. They can then use either their own or the real ending for their playmaking (but perhaps they could hear the real one at some point after they have made their own). This is interesting to do in groups so that the whole class can enjoy the different ideas.

The following two examples are included from a class of ten-year-olds who worked on this idea (the stories were written down after they had been acted). Description of character is just beginning, also the awareness of the value of surprise in drama, and need for some kind of an ending! (The same procedure can be adopted if central section or ending is the stimulus.)

> Suddenly there was a knock at the door. 'Oh crumbs what's that?' said Jimmy. 'I think someone knocked at the door' 'I'll answer' said John. So he crept towards the bedroom door, then opened it, and edged along to the front door. Pitter Patter went his bare feet down the staircase until he reached the door. Timidly he opened it and there stood a tough looking man, with an old ragged cap which was half over his eyes.
>
> 'W-w-what do you want', said John. 'I want money and jewels', said the man angrily. At this he pushed his way in and was just about to strike John, when his mother came in looking pleased with herself. 'Stop', she demanded, 'I've got a gun so don't move or I'll shoot'.
>
> It appeared that mother had met him before, so John got dressed and called the police, soon the man was taken away. So mother got an award which she shared with the family. Then they all sat down and laughed.
>
> (Sheila, aged 10)

> Suddenly there was a knock at the door I being the eldest said 'I'll get out of bed and see who it is'. knock! knock! so I called out 'allright im coming'. I opened the door there at the door was a dirty old tramp about 85 years old—cold, wet, and wearing a woollen helmet and gloves with the fingers out of, and he had a long beard. He looked as if he had never seen soap and water

before in his life. I didn't have the heart to send him away, so I called John he was very annoyed as he didn't like to leaved his cosy bed. I said 'Get this old man a nice warm drink. I went to the kitchenette to get a warm bowl of water a bar of soap and a flannel The tramp huddled up to the fire to get warm. I asked him what his name was he said 'Pepy is my name' I thought I regcognized the voice but could not place it. Then there was another knock it was mother she said 'Brr its cold' She came into the room. He took off his disguise and mummy said 'Tony' it was our father who had been lost for years.

(Bobbie, aged 10)

## Playwriting

The last two examples might almost be considered as the beginning of playwriting. Here are some other early attempts at recording dramatic experience by nine-year-olds, two during centre of interest work on whaling:

It happend one frosty mooning, so frosty that I could not see where I was going. As I was walking along the deck I herd somebody shouting for help so I ran to where the sound was coming from. When I got there I could see somethin wriggling about in the water it was one of our men. I ran for the life belt and I dropped it down into the the water. As I pulled him up he told me he had tripped over board in the frost I called for the the doctor and he was soon better. The frost cleared up and we were soon back to work.

*The Captain's Duties*

The Captain in a day has to fulfill a lot of of duties. (I play him.)
Captain (to Harpooner): Well, seen any whales?
Harpooner: Not yet sir.
Cook: Captain! Dinner's ready.
Spotter: Land ahoy sir!
Captain: Signal the engine room to stop.
First mate: Aye Aye sir.

Thirdly, a teacher went into a classroom during the lunch hour and found half-a-dozen boys engaged in the following play which they had thought up. Later they wrote it down.

*The Action takes place during a re-union of old friends at the school of their young days. It was also there that they used to meet as 'Cubs'.*

*Three old men enter with difficulty because of age and infirmity and sit on a desk. One suggests a song. 'My old man says follow the gun', is sung.*

*Enter 4th old man who says – 'That's old fashioned – I can sing some new words to the same tune'.*

*He proceeds to sing and dance in the fashion of an old man. He carries a box of tricks and says:* 'Shall we have some magic'. *Thy each take a card and he, with intense delight, is able to tell them the cards they have picked.*

1st OLD MAN: Shall we look at the photos on the wall and see if we can find a group of ourselves as cubs.

2nd OLD MAN: Yes, we're all here on the wall!

3rd OLD MAN: I wonder can you see the Cub Mistress – my eyes are very poor now.

5th OLD MAN: Yes, there she is – doesn't she look big and strong.

*Strange noises are now heard behind the board and easel and there emerges the 6th boy covered in a white sheet with slits for his eyes. He is the ghost of the Cub Mistress come to haunt them. He goes for each in turn and so terrorizes them that they all flee in terror followed by the ghost.*

## Drama from a piece of children's writing

Sometimes the teacher can use a piece of children's writing to initiate drama: this may or may not have been written for the purpose. The following is an example of a piece that was not written for drama. However the teacher was able to pick out the potentially exciting idea – that of the toy that has a life of its own and takes its owner on journeys to strange places and perhaps travels in strange ways. Interesting improvisation and sound accompaniment resulted.

> Once upon a time there was a boy called Timmy who lived in a house. He had no mother or father, sister or brother. He was seven years old. One day when he was walking down a road he saw a coin. He ran over the road and picked it up. The coin was a sixpence. He went round to a shop and bought a toy. When he got home he played with it, but when he put his hand on it, it went along and took Timmy along with it. When it stopped Timmy stopped. By then it was night so he went to bed.
>
> (Darren, aged 8)

### Drama from a picture

The teacher should collect pictures that appeal to the children and that imply clear situation and character. He can then stimulate drama by asking 'What is happening? What is he doing? What has been happening? Who else might come in/along? What will happen?' The children can then develop the ideas in group improvisation.

Sometimes children's drama work follows through into painting, but their paintings can also be used in the way suggested above, as stimuli for drama.

### Drama from an object

Both teacher and children can make a collection of objects which stimulate dramatic activity. A feather, an old coin, piece of an old letter, a piece of paper representing £1, a ring, a key, are all objects which have proved their worth in drama, to create situation. At first it is best to take one object and build up the atmosphere and situation with the children by asking questions about it:

'Where has it come from?'
'To whom does it belong?'
'Why does it look as it does?'
'What is it for?', etc.

The idea of the mysterious letter or part of a letter can be made more exciting if written on charred paper or as a secret message in some way, e.g. in code or milk on paper which is then warmed while damp to reveal the contents. (The milky letters turn brown.) Work with the whole class can develop from this, or the objects can be divided amongst smaller groups as a stimulus for playmaking. The object need not enter at the beginning – it might come later: why, with whom, it is by accident?, etc.

### Drama from costume

In the Infant School it is usual to see dressing-up going on in the corner of the room, or in the corridor, and many infant teachers keep a well-stocked dressing-up box or rack in their rooms. However there are only rare chances for this activity in Junior Schools, so the occasional use of items of clothing or material such as an old fur coat, a blanket, a scarlet cloak, sundry interesting hats, a large pair of boots, a helmet, a pair of glasses, a false nose, an animal mask, a beard, a wig or two can provide a stimulating opportunity. This is usually best undertaken by a group of children at a time, while the rest of the class are busy on other work. Alternatively divide the class into groups and give each three items to use. Use materials too such as boxes, paper bags, newspaper.

## Use of available space: hall or classroom

The most convenient place for doing work such as described in this handbook is in a hall or large space out of sight and earshot of as much of the rest of the school as possible and without the disturbance of passers-by or passers-through. However, since there is often a gulf between the desirable and achievable in this as in other school matters, first some comments on the use of the classroom for drama. Since the aim is still to have every class member 'doing' in some way for most of the time, select topics and organize furniture accordingly (e.g. to the sides of the room). In the classroom, it is mainly extended use of floor patterns, wide stretching movements by many children at once and group movement in general which have to be curtailed. Movement on the spot, sitting, and kneeling can be achieved, and it is a good idea to suggest and encourage the invention of themes and stories which by their nature keep two-thirds or three-quarters of the class on the spot or comparatively static, while the others move. Even within these limitations make varied use of the space. The more static group can be in clumps (e.g. towers or frightened groups), lines (e.g. walls, human barriers) or triangular wedge, broken half-circle, close square or circle, for reasons of the drama content. Levels can be varied from group to group and within groups. Clear and varied use can be made of focus (and changes of direction) on something imagined far away, perhaps watching an object or person travelling around the sky or horizon.

Children can continue improvisation and playmaking even if only a confined space is available and can often use settings which are spatially limited and ideal for classroom work. Examples include: in a spacecraft, aeroplane, submarine, bus, car, lorry, train, tube train, lift, ship's cabin, well, secret passage, tunnel, hole in the road, sand pit, chasm, hollow tree, lifeboat, rowing boat, canoe, pothole, cave, mine, igloo, tent, cage, prison, cupboard, bank, vault, chair watching TV, kiosk or chair using telephone, signal box, office, shop, chimney, alley or crowded place, etc. Sometimes the hall can seem too large for action in scenes such as these. Remember also it can be easier for the beginner to initiate and organize drama in the classroom than in a larger space where control and observation are more difficult and a dictatorial manner too easily assumed.

Also in the classroom, children can create radio programmes of many kinds and make and use puppets. Topics demanding discussion and other specific speech work including the enjoyment of poetry and story telling will also be taking place.

However, if a hall or larger space is available make full use of the opportunities it gives for movement, especially group work and journeys. From the middle of the Infant School upwards, make increasing use of rostrum blocks and steps scattered over the floor and forming locales. Even if there is a stage in the hall, all-round playing rather than proscenium acting should be encouraged. Sometimes with older children, the stage can be used like an outsize rostrum block for one of the locales, provided there is easy access to it from the floor of the hall where the main action should continue to take place.

## Titles, scenes or incidents: for individual or partner work, or small groups

The children must have experienced, observed, or be able to imagine easily a comparable incident/person/animal in real life.

> We should attempt to train children, as far as we can, to see as well as to look, to hear as well as to listen, to observe with knowledge and imagination; to perceive, to relate, to associate. As a result of such training in accurate observation and reflection on that observation, in the recording in language of that observation and reflection particularly by simile, metaphor and imagery, some children who do not already possess them may acquire the 'seeing eye' and 'hearing ear' as well as some facility for perceiving relationships and associations.[1]

Buying shoes/hats/food/car
At the newsagents (a complaint perhaps connected with the delivery boy)
A mimed action by one or more children, others join in to create a scene
A bus journey real or fantastic (e.g. a bus that grows wings)
A telephone call
Watching TV
Felling trees
Seaside: contrast a hot day with a cold or wet day
Spring-cleaning

Helping a blind person
Shipwreck
Family car-ride (a puncture? Something or someone has been left at home?)
Haunted house
Trip to the Zoo
Jungle
Going out into the snow
The picnic (cows arrive unexpectedly?)
In a self-service store (pile of tins knocked over)
A country walk (rain storm)
In a factory
Train journey (loss of ticket)
Flying a kite (tangled in tree or lost)
Guide and sightseers
A misunderstanding
A quarrel
An argument
A difficult interview
Interviewing a famous person
A journalist gets a scoop for his paper
A deep sea diver meets trouble
Putting up a tent in calm or stormy conditions
Nightmare
The hole in the road
The fire
On a building site
The return of the lifeboat

## For larger groups or the whole class

At railway station, air port, bus station, sports ground, seaside, fair, circus; in a park, café, shops; on the scene of a crime; watching an air display, a football match, the boat race, a cliff rescue; listening for a signal, for footsteps, for a car, for the telephone; smelling gas, fire; passing different imaginary objects round, a bomb, hot plate, an injured cat, something prickly, a feather, a huge parcel – with or without saying what the object is; or something magic that keeps changing its shape, texture, temperature, character. Following the leader; the escape; smugglers, robots, explorers; bringing news.

## Characters to develop

(Develop means reveal specific characteristics, mood, action and reasons for action and mood changes, invent an incident.)

Highwayman
Nightwatchman
Inefficient shop assistant
Ghost
Tyrannical ruler
Foolish servant
Clumsy burglar
Cowardly poacher
Worried mother
Effusive person
Shy person
Dominating person
Nervous person

In twos or threes different characters can meet each other, then in different situations. Then different groups of characters can meet. Then different feelings can be added, e.g. resentment, anger, fear, excitement, dislike, surprise, great haste, of being overlooked, of being up against authority.

Work of this kind may induce fighting. 'An eye for an eye, a tooth for a tooth' is a typical attitude of Primary Children. Their natural response to violence of any kind is a physically violent one and part of their everyday lives. The teacher must therefore expect to find this natural response to certain stimuli during creative activity. It is important not to repress or curtail this happening although if handled incompetently, distressing discipline difficulties occur. A sensitive approach and careful preparation of suitable stimuli can assist by making purposeful use of this fighting instinct that exists, especially in boys. The following suggestions may help to channel children's energies into constructive imaginative directions.

Fighting can be disciplined, timed and with older children, structured. It can be done in slow motion for some reason, e.g. because of magic, being under water or in space, wearing heavy armour, adversaries having barrier between – river, wall. It can be stylized to drum, or cymbal beats, using imaginary long swords, with a definite sequence of moves: to, away, around, past, beyond an opponent. Stories for drama can be chosen or made which include fights which are disciplined or limited in some way as indicated above. If horseplay gets too violent, one way of curbing this is to point out there is no relation between it and the story and another way is to provide plenty of energetic opportunities in the drama session.

Characters can be made up who, because of their nature, bring about situations, action, reaction and adventure. Fantasy creatures such as Daleks who have super-human power can be thought of; incredible journeys can thus be undertaken.

A child can only fully create or experience a character when he understands that character in relation to himself. He also needs to be able to visualize the appearance of the character, what he is wearing, imagine the colour, weight, and texture of the clothes. Then, of course, he needs to work his way into the kinds of everyday actions this character performs, and his personal way of behaviour. He needs, too, to imagine he is at the home or job of this person, and can pretend to arrange the room or shop or wherever it is. He may then be ready to receive another character and have a conversation exchange. If he has a shop, perhaps the second character has come in to buy something for a special occasion and needs advice; so, briefly, to work in characterization we need to focus on how he/she/it looks, how he/she/it moves, what he/she/it does in various situations. The teacher should be careful to discourage 'ham' or 'type' acting of characters by helping the children to deepen their understanding of any specific character, to make it an individual and to feel personal concern for it. Some characteristics come from age, some from mood, some from condition, others from situation. Any movement results from the character's feeling or instinct or ideas, (feelings such as: fear, anger, disgust, tenderness, distress, loneliness, curiosity; or escaping, aggressive, hoarding, protective instincts).

These two children were just beginning the process of 'getting into character' when they dictated the following:

> I am Pharoah King of Egypt. I wear robes and jewels. I am very important to the country of which I rule. My job is to help save Egypt from any foe or enemy. I can do almost anything I like. I am a very rich and proud type of person, I have servants, maids and butlers to wait on me. Everybody in Egypt is under my power. I order all my servants to do their work. I can put people in prison when I like and as long as I like. When people enter my court they must bow before me.
>
> (Janet, aged 8)

I am the jailor. I am fat I have feet that make my shoes sound heavy when I walk. I am not very young. . . . . I wear a belt from which the prison keys hang. . . . I wear black trousers with a stripe at the side to show that I'm a jailor. . . . .

(Sandra, aged 8½)

Children can suggest characters they want in their play, and contribute observations of both people and animals.

Examples such as the following led to the class development of a street scene.

*A Journey to School*

On my way to school we pass a public house called the Dew Drop. There is often an old dirty lady waiting outside the public house – She waits from 9 o'clock till about 11 o'clock. She wears an old dirty fur coat with the tuck and the linen hanging down. She also wears a pair of odd earing too.

We also pass a bakers' and they make there own bread and cakes. They are called Hemmings and a man who drives the bread to different shops, always shouts to us 'Hurry up ladies or you will be late for school'. He is a tall broad man with an oldish face with a moustache.

(Pat, aged 10)

Up Brixton there is an old lady and she sells newspapers. Her hair is a greyish white, her skin is wrinkled she has an old hat on her head, she wears a dirty fur coat, with a long dirty torn dress that reaches her ankles. She has big black bags under her feeble looking eyes. She wears dirty holey white plimsols, she is very dirty she is about ninety! And there she sits huddled up on a little stool.

(Jacquelyn, aged 10)

Another approach to character is to focus on hands, making them take on different characteristics: nervous, greedy, flabby, magic, fierce, gentle, strong, frightened, etc. While working on hands it will be seen the whole child is involved without realizing it. Individual or group work developing one of these ideas can follow. (Also try working on feet or elbows.)

## Characterization and situation from a newspaper headline or news item

The class or group considers the headline or news item for drama potential and enacts the results.

One headline used in this way was: MAYOR CLIMBS TOWN HALL

CLOCK TOWER. Why did he climb it? When? Was he alone: What happened? (The actual report could be kept secret until after the improvisation.)

A news item used was: 'The Escape of an animal from the Zoo'. This stimulated many reactions: Zoo officials, Zoo keeper, bystanders, people living near the park where animal was thought to be, other animals, parliament, park-keeper, RSPCA officials, the foreign dignatory who presented the animal to the Zoo, unscrupulous furriers, a foreign spy.

## Characterization and situation from a ballad or song

The method for using this suggestion is similar to that used for the nursery rhyme example in Chapter 4. Here, however, with older children, the content and development can be more challenging.

Songs which can be used in this way include sea shanties, Negro spirituals, cowboy songs, railroad songs, folk songs. For example: Casey Jones, The Lincolnshire Poacher, King Arthur's Men, Jericho, Agincourt Song, Henry Martin, Barbara Allen.

## Fantasy characters/scenes

Fantasy characters and scenes are often included in nightmare or life in other worlds. Music is helpful in stimulating work of this nature, also poetry including the children's own poems. The following poems on the colour black by three eleven-year-olds, arising from a class discussion on colours, give ideas for fantasy drama.

Black is the werewolf and vampire Dracula crawling through
the dingey dank night. It is also the swish of the
bat's wing and the colour of Batman's cape and car.
Black is a burnt rice pudding made by an amateur cook.
Black is black as Los Bravos says.
My shoes are black, they are chisel toed, slip ons.
Our carpet at home is black.
Jet black is a powder colour and the rim of Gillian
Slater's glasses. Black is a never ending fall
through time.
The infinite void of space is black.
Black is the face of a sweep and black is a mole in a
deep, dark hole.

(Christopher)

Black is the colour of dead dull night,
A skeleton lying in your bed.
Figures of a ghostly phantom,
Coal is black and black is black.
Burnt things are black.
Black is a devilish colour,
A tree with no life in it.
Black is a graveyard,
Someone in dismay,
A horrible feeling,
Someone rising from the dead.
A black cat.
Black faces or legs when we've been playing,
Mischievous,
People's eyeballs,
Black ugly teeth,
A dentist's chair,
Tombs of dead people
Someone in a coma,
Smells of poison gas,
A deafening whistle.
Dreams are black like an empty mind.
Miners are black.
Silence is an ugly black.

(Anette)

Non existence is black.
Black is the dead of night.
Mr. Smith's pit boots are black
Malaria is black death.
Black is the foghorn's shout.
Terror is black.
Black is the middle of grief.
Awkwardly means black.
Black means contraband
Black, the colour of school blazers.
Jungle's depth is like the black night
Pit miners faces are black.
Shadows lazily are dead.
Skulls are the black of death.
The panther's pounce is black.

(Kenneth)

Sometimes, in a class drama session, the teacher will want to give experience in a variety of situations and characters. This can be great fun and means the child is learning to be versatile and quick thinking. It means his dramatic imagination has to work fast. However, if the teacher is not careful, the result of this lesson pattern can be a series of superficial little 'mimes', totally unrelated to each other or to drama, and offering scant opportunity for creative development of any one idea. It is not always even clear whether occupational, character, or symbolic 'mime' is required. The child does not know whether to re-act as himself in the various situations, or whether he can pretend to be someone else. Motivation, a clear necessity in drama, is often non-existent. The child is initiated into a series of unrelated reactions. He is waiting for the stimulus from the teacher each time: his focus and attention will be constantly brought back to the teacher. The force of the teacher's personality, the fact that out of so many suggestions some of the children will be able to respond at least some of the time, and simple enjoyment of moving in the space, can make such a lesson an apparent success. But is it a real success? At its worst or even best, the drama experience is equivalent to being at a party and trying on a series of different hats in quick succession.

If the teacher is dissatisfied with this pattern, and yet wants to continue a series of brief mimes throughout the lesson (the versatility, etc., may be his immediate aim), one solution is to take one character through a variety of situations. Alternatively one can approach the same problem, situation or character from different points of view.

## Themes

Another idea is to take a potent theme such as Air, Fire, Earth or Water and to investigate this in dramatic terms.

For example, Water. One aspect of this topic could include the sea. (Children who have never seen the sea will of course need special consideration.)

### I. *Stimuli*

Poems about the sea from School anthologies and extracts from other sources such as:

It keeps eternal whisperings round
Desolate shores, and with its mighty swell
Gluts twice ten thousand cavers.
(Keats)

To the deep, to the deep
Down down
Through the grey void abysm
Down down
Where the air is no prism
And the moon and stars are not
And the cavern crags wear not the radiance of heaven
To the deep to the deep
Down down.
(Shelley)

And sudden dark a patch of sea was shaded
And sudden light another patch would hold
The warmth of whirling atoms in a sunshot
And underwater sandstorm green and gold.
(Betjeman)

Rain patterns on a sea that tilts and sighs
Fast-running floors, collapsing into hollows,
Tower suddenly, spray-haired. Contrariwise,
A wave drops like a wall; another follows,
Wilting and scrambling, timelessly at play
Where there are no ships and no shallows
(Larkin)

What dreadful noise of waters in my ears
What sights of ugly death within my eyes!
Methoughts I saw a thousand fearful wrecks
A thousand men that fishes gnawed upon.
Wedges of gold, great anchors, heaps of pearl,
Inestimable stones, unvalued jewels
All scattered in the bottom of the sea.
Some lay in dead mens skulls, and in the holes
Where eyes did once inhabit there were crept
As twere in scorn of eyes, reflecting gems
That woo'd the slimy bottom of the deep
And mocked the dead bones that lay scattered by.
(Shakespeare)

Full fathom five thy father lies;
Of his bones are coral made;
Those are pearls that were his eyes
Nothing of him that doth fade,
But doth suffer a sea change
Into something rich and strange.
Sea nymphs hourly ring his knell:
Ding dong
Hark! now I hear them
Ding dong bell.
(Shakespeare)

Sand-strewn caverns, cool and deep,
Where the winds are all asleep;
Where the spent lights quiver and gleam;
Where the salt weeds sway in the stream;
Where the sea beasts ranged all round
Feed in the ooze of their pasture ground;
Where the sea snakes coil and twine;
Dry their mail and bask in the brine.
Where great whales come sailing by;
Sail and sail with unshut eye,
Round the world for ever and aye.
(Arnold)

2. *Music* such as:
Holst: *The Planets:* 'Neptune'; 'Saturn'
Ravel: *Daphnis and Chloe*
Bartok: *Music for strings, percussion and celeste*
Britten: *Sea interludes*

3. *Pictures*
(a) reproductions and photographs collected from papers and magazines
(b) children's own pictures.

4. *Features: ideas*
Caves, seashore: cliffs, tides, smugglers
Life in the sea, real or imaginary
Legends concerned with the sea
The great days of sail

Scavengers of flotsam and jetsam
Fishermen
Storm
Shipwreck
Treasure
Lighthouse
Deep sea divers
Pirates
Fishermen, fishing ballads
Sailors, sea shanties
Sea journeys, e.g. Kon Tiki, Jonah and the whale,
Odysseys; lone rowers/sailors.

And from literature, for teachers' use or as extracts for the older children —

e.g. *The Ancient Mariner,* Coleridge
*Moby Dick*, Herman Melville
*The Old Man of the Sea*, Hemingway
*Youth*, Joseph Conrad

If a theme such as this is chosen, there might be a particular historical event associated with it which could give rise to drama.

To take another example, if 'Fire' was chosen, the Great Fire of London is an obvious event, especially to London children. A visit to the London Museum could be incorporated into the study or even initiate it. Success of the drama in such a venture depends largely on how steeped the children can become in the atmosphere, facts, likely characters and events. The children should be allowed to discover objects in a museum for themselves, to form their own impressions. On the spot sketches can be made, and written notes if not too laborious an undertaking. (Spoken comments may be more beneficial.) Perhaps answers to questions such as the following could be collected and discussed. (Museum room numbers are added for the benefit of those who can use the Museum.)

*Model of the Great fire*: *Room 14*

1. Can you see why the fire spread easily?
2. Say what you think people placed in the boats.
3. Name any important building that was burned.
4. Write down the number of houses destroyed.

5. Can you suggest where the homeless would go?
6. Do you think the streets would really be empty like this?
7. Make a list of four animals that might be caught in the fire.

*Fighting the Great Fire: Room 14a*

8. Look for a fireman's helmet. What is it made of?
9. Say what the big brim was for.
10. Draw the helmet on the back of this paper.
11. Look for a handsquirt and find out how many men were needed to work it.
12. Would the water from the squirt reach the roof-tops?
13. How would they put out blazing thatch!
14. What were fire-buckets made of?
15. Sketch a bucket on the back of the paper.

*Painting of the Great Fire: Room 17*

16. Which bridge is shown?
17. Say in whose shop the fire began.
18. Explain why the fire spread quickly westwards
19. What is the pale grey building on the right.
20. We do not know the name of the artist. Can you find in which country he was trained?
21. Make any drawing you would like for your book in school.

The children can pretend they are living at the time of the Great Fire. They can describe who they are, what job they have and what happens to them during the fire. Perhaps they have ideas for drama. The teacher can read descriptions from literature to the class, such as this extract from John Evelyn's diary: 'God grant mine eyes may never behold the like, who now saw above 10,000 houses all in one flame! The noise and cracking and thunder of the impetuous flames, the shrieking of women and children, the hurry of people, the fall of towers, houses, and churches was like a hideous storm!'

In preparation for building drama scenes, the teacher may find *The Plague and Fire of London*[2] and *London's Burning*[3] helpful.

BOOK REFERENCES

1. Alington, A. F., *Drama and Education*, Blackwell.
2. *The Plague and Fire of London*, Jackdaw Series, Jonathan Cape.
3. John Bedford, *London's Burning*, Abelard-Schuman

# Chapter 6: The Use and Development of Sound and Speech

## Use of Sound

Encourage the children to become more aware of everyday sounds and of the differences between them. How can they be described? (The children can close their eyes and listen to the sounds of the school and near environment, they can try to distinguish the sounds and imagine what or who is making them.)

Exploration of sounds from different sources: (a) physical (b) domestic (c) percussion (d) conventional melodic instruments

(a) *Physical*
(i) vocal (see Speech section)
(ii) feet on floor, hand claps, hands on knees, floor, etc., finger clicks
(iii) other human sounds such as: sneeze, cough, laugh, sing, whistle, 'Ugh!' 'Mmm'.

(b) *Domestic*
Such as small objects in different securely-fastened containers, e.g. stones, rice, nutmegs, paper clips, curtain rings on different rods and wires; glasses/bowls of water to strike; jugs to call into; bottles to blow into; elastic bands to pluck; an old typewriter; rotary egg whisk; wire egg slicer (to pluck); paper being torn or crumpled; hairbrush stroked across basket; thimbled fingers tapping on different surfaces; chains of various thickness (dragged, dropped on floor); marble rolling round a circular tray, tin or tambour; clay flower pots of different sizes hung up with string and struck (preferably using a hard rubber headed beater) stones of different sizes striking against each other to make a note (also hard woods in the same way).

(c) *Percussion*
A collection such as the following should be gradually built up: drums,

including African, Chinese, Israeli; tuneable tambours, woodblocks and sticks; chime bars; xylophones: bass, alto, soprano; glockenspiels; bass, alto, soprano (the pentatonic scale is sufficient to begin with); cymbals for use with a beater; gongs; a variety of beaters with different sized heads; heads of felt, rubber, wood and wire brushes. For helpful advice on making instruments, see *Make Your Own Musical Instruments!*[1]

(d) *Conventional Melodic Instruments*
Use as available.

Work with all these sounds is needed in drama, from time to time. In addition, children can develop their ideas by working on several sound pictures, perhaps imagining these as part of a radio play: e.g. a volcano, a haunted house, the sea, the jungle, a farm, things cooking, a clockmaker's shop, machines, a battle, etc.

The teacher also uses sound to stimulate and support the dramatic activity. (See section on infant drama from sounds.) One approach with older infants and juniors is to play a sequence of sounds to the class and ask them to imagine this as part of a film, TV or radio sound track. Having imagined the scene, the people, the things associated with the sounds, ask the class to imagine they are part of this scene themselves. (They will need to hear the sequence several times, repeated exactly.) If they have imagined a sea scene including a boat, for instance, they could pretend they are in that boat, or underneath it. Where are they going? Why? Perhaps they may be escaping or chasing or exploring or searching. Perhaps they are a smuggler or a spy. Encourage development by further provoking questions, 'What would happen if. . . .?' (e.g. if a storm blew up, or the boat sprang a leak, or the boat was not his, or fog descends).

As usual, the purpose is stimulation and development of the children's ideas.

## Using recorded music

Here the choice of music presents the first problem, and the introduction and development of the idea with the class, the second. To deal with the second: it is dubious practice to impose any one 'picture' on a class, supposedly arising from a piece of music. However, if specifically descriptive 'programme' music is chosen, the children can be encouraged to pretend they see a moving picture as the music progresses. The teacher

| Title of Music and Composer | Dominant Instruments | Volume and Intensity Mainly | Tempo Mainly | Melody Mainly | Leads to Drama–Movement possibilities such as: |
|---|---|---|---|---|---|
| | (Teachers can fill in these first two columns according to the music chosen) | Strong | Slow | Direct* | Grand processions, royalty, power, dignity, deliberate movement, frightening effects, squeezing, pulling actions. |
| | | Strong | Slow | Twisting | Powerful plotting, witches, twisted, tortuous, knotted movement, frightening effects, gnarled shapes. |
| | | Strong | Quick | Direct | Action, business, battle, confident, tough characteristics |
| | | Strong | Quick | Twisting | Storm, rash anger, whipping battle, scattering movements. |
| | | Less | Slow | Direct | Hypnotic, gliding, ghosts, stealthy, calm, lingering |
| | | Less | Slow | Twisting | Wafting, vaporous, sinister, eerie |
| | | Less | Quick | Direct | Darting, dodging, bright, light-hearted, crowd scene, busy, panic |
| | | Less | Quick | Twisting | Thoughtless, frivolous, fussy, sparkling, erratic, nervous |
| | | | Generally heavy | | Plodding, working, depression |
| | | | Generally repetitive rhythm | | Machines, boredom, 'in the power of' |

* By 'Direct' I mean a melody which moves in step by step progression, or is composed mainly of held notes, or has phrases consisting of several notes travelling down or up in a phrase. (These suggestions are based on my application of Rudolph Laban's Principles and Practice of Movement.)

should have definite questions ready to assist aural focus and concentration and to stimulate imagination and movement ideas. Suggestions can be given and collected from the children on the possible situation and atmosphere at the start, and activities that might be going on. Direct questions about the music can be posed, such as, 'What did you feel/think when you heard. . . . .?' 'What did the . . . . . . . . . sound make you do?' 'Did you hear the . . . . . . .?' Through repeating the music, allow the children to get adequate knowledge of it. Also, make sure they know the title of the piece they are using.

Another legitimate use of music is as an aid to atmosphere, or mood, as used in film, TV or radio play background.

Sound effects records should also be used. In general, if starting from a piece of music, or if looking for a piece for a dance-drama or as a background for a drama sequence, aim as far as possible for mood and rhythm content. It may be helpful to classify the music and resultant drama possibilities as page 61; music for each of the ten categories is often needed, therefore worth collecting.

## Speech

Two little dogs sat by the fire
Over a fender of coal dust;
Said one little dog to the other little dog,
If you don't talk, why, I must.

Children's speech: what are the teacher's aims here? Certainly not to give children skill in talking for the sake of talking, or in filling silence, as indicated above. Of course we want them to have an adequate vocabulary, and fluency, ease and confidence when they speak, with clear articulation and enunciation (which means, consonants and vowels produced efficiently). But they first need something to talk about and the wish to talk about it. Listening is important too; as Rottlisburger says, 'The biggest block to personal communication is man's inability to listen intelligently, understandingly and skilfully to another person.'

Something to talk about: life is full of events that cause speech and some of these take place in school or are discussed in school. Language gives shape to an experience, to a reaction. Often the act of speaking itself is a reaction to a new experience. Sometimes the speaking is not about the experience, it is simply a release of feeling. Children do not need or wish to talk about everything they do. However, they are likely to have plenty to say about a specific topic if it interests them, and they use language as well as play to master their environment. 'We learn to see a thing by learning to describe it' (Raymond Williams)[2] and an experience is not fully realized until it is described.

Talking about something does not automatically mean that communication is taking place. For communication to be successful, adequate description is needed. One of our aims is of course to help children to widen their vocabulary and use of words, so that they will be able to communicate satisfactorily in life situations. To quote M. M. Lewis, 'as he passes from infancy to childhood the possibilities of his further development depends more and more upon his mastery of language as a more sensitive, more refined and more finely-adjusted instrument of communication and thought.'[3] Children need to be able to explain their ideas and actions and to understand the explanations given by others. 'The capacity to make a meaning plain should be the first goal the Junior School teacher sets for the children' (HMSO report).[4]

Of course we know that schools and teachers are not the chief influences in this matter. 'Language development depends on the general level of English in the home. Research shows that children of the same age or about the same intelligence, coming from homes of widely different cultural levels and opportunities, may differ by as much as three years in vocabulary, so great is the force of environment'.[5] Language development is also influenced by inherited and instinctive drives, and by other children. Children evolve their own language for communication with each other and also use chants and slogans for this purpose. 'Studies in the development of children's language show how closely it is related to their other learning in becoming social with other children through conversation and argument, in asking questions of adults and adding to their store of information explaining what they want and how they feel, forming concepts.'[6]

How does a child learn to speak? By listening, by imitation, by association, by using language, by being given helpful correction. As teachers we are interested in the chants and slogans of the playground, but our job is to help the child cope with language and speech in other situations. We aim to save him from the frustrations of being inarticulate. Vague words mean and lead to vague thought, and language facility aids the recall and manipulation of past experiences; a required process of reasoning ability is to develop. Moreover, as Aldous Huxley writes in *Words and their Meanings*, 'conduct and character are largely determined by the nature of the words we currently use to discuss ourselves and the world around us.'[7]

Clearly, all this gives the teacher considerable responsibility. How can initiating drama with his class assist him? As should be apparent in previous chapters, in the drama situation, conversation, discussion, with individuals and in both small and large groups, is a purposeful necessity. Teachers beginning drama teaching may find they have to work at this technique. To achieve success with individual children, bear in mind the following quotation about Harold Williamson: 'If he has a secret, it may be in his sensitive appreciation of the uniqueness of his encounter with each child'.[8]

A start can be made by asking questions and by not accepting perfunctory answers. We can initiate children's thinking in drama by the nature of the questions we ask. If a child answers only in monosyllables perhaps the question needs re-framing. Through our questions we can cause the child to examine situation and character deeply, to examine and speak about problems. This becomes an even more important function of drama at the Secondary stage.

The drama situation affords the teacher opportunity for selecting and presenting literature to the children, as stimulus or ancillary material. Skilful reading aloud can bring an increased awareness of function, power and beauty of language to children. Also, the love of word sounds and language patterns which we have observed in the playground is needed and encouraged in drama. This feeling for language was described by T. S. Eliot as 'auditory imagination': 'the feeling for syllable and rhythm, penetrating far below the conscious levels of thought and feeling, invigorating every word; sinking to the most primitive and forgotten, returning to the origin and bringing something back, seeking the beginning and the end.'[9]

Vocal sounds or words are sometimes needed in drama as accompaniment. Children can explore this possibility and make up words of their own too. A monster makes a noise: several children speaking simultaneously make their own phrases from words such as: snarl, squelch, sting, ooze, whiffle, scrunch, varying the length of words and using repetition. Magic words to make certain things happen, and witches' spells that usually do likewise, are sometimes needed. Narration has to be made from time to time. Perhaps the sky palace has to be described and children can search for appropriate words: dazzling, shimmering, glowing, glimmering, shining, silvery, vivid, sparkling, etc.; or the old hag's cave: gloomy, dim, smoky, dismal, clammy, dreary, dank, drab, dark, spooky, shadowy, slimy, deathly, etc.

Perhaps the narrator(s) describe(s) how the different people and animals make a journey chasing the villain into the sky: they amble, they crawl, they creep, they slide, they slither, they stalk, they sneak, they squirm; they amble, they totter, they shuffle, they writhe; they (and very fast) run, dodge, hop, skip, gallop, bound, frisk, prance, trip, stride, jump, leap – FLY!

The rhythmic use of words can be helpful in working-action scenes.

Children can improve the expressive quality of their speech by matching the sounds of their words to accompanying mood music or sound. For instance, the witches try to make their voices like the rasping noise provided as accompaniment.

Through work such as this, though without necessarily telling them so, the children have all been practising, enjoying and, we hope, improving articulation, enunciation, projection. They have been given contrasting opportunities for vocal sound and speech, needing variety of pitch, tone, pace and emphasis. They have extended both vocabulary and use of words.

However, drama needs more than words, phrases and pieces of narration. In drama, the child should find himself in a wide range of situations, all requiring specific vocal response. This response might begin as grunts, gasps, whistles, mutterings, but will develop into the use of words. One of the teacher's aims is to encourage the selection and use of appropriate words: speech appropriate to the situation; and this ability should be fostered by role playing. A language can only become really meaningful in situations, and can only be practised satisfactorily in situations, real or imaginary.

In Junior Schools, when there is five or ten minutes to spare, children can try one of the following suggestions: (Teachers should of course add to these lists.)

*In one minute*

Name as many goods as you can in the supermarket (or local shop)
Describe a cat (or other animal)
(girls) Explain how to knit

(boys) Explain goal-keeper's job
Describe how to boil an egg
Name everything in the room without stopping
(Teacher or child produces an object) Talk about this
Explain how to get from the classroom to the playground
Explain how to get to the nearest bus stop/railway station
'What I like to eat'
Imagine you are watching a building on fire and tell us about it
Explain a proverb or phrase (e.g. to put the cart before the horse)
Explain the difference between two or more nearly related objects (e.g. gloves/mittens; bed/hammock/bunk/fourposter/cot
Why do leaves fall in Autumn?
(Teacher or child gives a message or shopping list) Repeat this correctly
Imagine you are in a phone kiosk and explain how you make a call
With a partner, improvise dialogue for a mimed scene (performed by two different children)
Describe a local building
Describe something in the room
Give a running commentary on an imaginary sporting event (e.g. football match, swimming gala).

*In no more than three minutes* (this can be prepared in advance)
Pretend you are making an invention, talk about it as you make it and then describe it to us. (Alternatively, with a partner, one makes, one describes)
Talk about a topic, or describe a place or something of your own choice (and answer questions afterwards).

*If more time is available.*
Have a 'Lucky Dip': children speak on whatever they draw out (class or groups). Ideas game (see Chapter 4) or story round the room each child adding a word or phrase. And for an extended speech and drama topic, a radio programme.

**About Louis Braille: Inventor at Fifteen**
References are to the biography of Louis Braille by G. Webster, *Journey into Light*. There is also a book suitable for children called *The Young Louis Braille* by Clare H. Abrahall published by Max Parrish.

The theme has considerable possibilities for radio playwork by top junior children. There is scope for varied background work and optional use of French for those schools where it is in the curriculum.

*Brief notes on the life of Louis Braille*

He was born in 1809 in Coupray, a village outside Paris, when France was in the turmoil of the Napoleonic Wars. He had devoted and sensible parents, the father a harness maker much respected in his locality. Louis, youngest of four, totally blinded himself by a childish accident at three years old. The family home was a single-roomed stone cottage amidst vineyards and fields. At the age of seven he had the opportunity, rare for a blind child, to attend the village school through the help of the local Curé. Louis listened, and remembered, often reaching first place in his class. Through the initiative of his father, strongly supported by the Curé, he went at ten to the National Institute for Blind Youth in Paris, little knowing that apart from holidays, he would remain there all his life, a pupil, then a teacher and musician, with one absorbing concern above all others.

*Stages in his life at the Institute*

(a) It began with disillusion
(b) He made friends, won prizes, began to love music, learned to play the piano and later the organ and at fourteen was made 'foreman' at the Institute workshop where the students made slippers. But in all spare time during the day, and often in the night, he worked to find a new way for the blind to read. At fifteen he found it. He had invented a new alphabet, one for the blind; in course of time it was to bring untold enrichment to the lives of blind people throughout the world.
(c) He became a teacher, and an organist and pianist with many engagements.
(d) At last in 1844, at the opening of the new building for the Institute, came the first public recognition of the value of his work.

*Suggestions for Dramatic Work*

The teacher may wish to discuss with the children attitudes to the blind, now and in the past. They may be encouraged to imagine a life without colour – or light for a child who can never run freely in town or countryside. In the following scene emphasis is laid (by the action) on an opinion widely held not so long ago, that the blind not only lack sight – but normal wits as well. It is set in Paris, 1771, and an authentic story is the basis of the action.[10]

*'Café des Aveugles'*

The known facts are as follows: A World Fair was held in Paris in 1871. There was a café in the town called 'Café des Aveugles' where the special attraction was a mock orchestra of ten blind men, wearing dunces' caps with asses' ears attached, pretending to play old broken-down instruments. They had large cardboard spectacles. The leader (not blind) waved a broom as a baton, and now and again slapped one of the players with it – to the accompaniment of roars of laughter from the spectators, who raised their glasses and banged their tankards on the tables. One man watched this with increasing distress and anger; he was Valentin Huay, visitor to the Fair. That very day he decided to found a school for the blind where they would learn to read; none existed at the time. (It was in fact the Institute where Louis spent most of his life.)

*Suggestions for the Scene. Outside a café, bearing in large letters the name 'Café des Aveugles'.* (Some children may know a little French and enjoy using it.)

A gay mood prevails; people are sitting, some with children, at the tables outside. Tourists come along, some stop to look at the notice. A French–English conversation begins. A Frenchman with characteristic gestures says with a laugh that 'L'Orchestre' will soon arrive. Some strange sounds are heard and the orchestra and leader come in (as described above). They 'perform'. Passers-by stop and watch, among them Valentin Huay. The usual hilarity is shown. An interruption occurs; along the street comes a man ringing a bell. He announces a special event at the Fair (perhaps an Acrobat Display, a famous Clown . . .). People move off, 'orchestra' goes in. Valentin Huay, sickened, sits at a table. A couple notice this, offer help – talk follows and he expresses his views with passionate feeling. The idea of teaching the blind to read is born.

Here are some suggestions for dramatizing scenes in Louis Braille's life; they are mainly short scenes with simple backgrounds:

*Louis' early life*
The teacher gives background of his life in the village. It is 1816, with France in great distress following the Napoleonic defeat. Various incidents for possible dramatization are suggested in the biography.

*Last day at home*
Mother dominates the scene. She bustles about getting Louis ready for departure, and preparing meal. Neighbours come in, lively talk goes on. Louis, excited, tells them of the school uniform he will wear with gold buttons. Father reminds them, the coach may be on time! Farewells are said. Mother reminds Louis of the fine parcel of food, with a whole chicken, she has packed.

*First Day at National Institute for Blind Youth*
The teacher gives comments on the Institute, an old damp building with dormitories and in them iron bedsteads. There are sixty pupils, all blind of course, mainly in their teens. Louis is ten, the youngest. For him the all-important thing is that he will learn to read and so enter the magic world of books. He is totally unprepared for the realities he faces in the first few weeks.

The teacher gives description of interview at the Institute. Father is with the boy, is told of arrangements. Louis loses his precious parcel of food, put carefully under his bed, which he hoped to share with his new friend, Jean. Later he is bullied by bigger school boys and street louts. These authentic facts are used in the next two scenes.[11]

*A Rough Beginning*
(a) A lesson is just ending. Big boys gather round Louis, tease him with hints of initiation tests for new boys, laugh at his accent. Jean, accustomed to going out by himself invites Louis to go with him, to get away from the bullies.
(b) In a street outside a shop. Louis and Jean are talking, Louis has some money, says he will buy some iced cake. They go in, a kindly woman serving, helps them. No sooner are they out than other boys snatch the cakes, taunt them with blindness, and throw some rubbish at them. They stumble away in wild distress. Louis says he will go back to the shop, ask the woman to help him write a letter asking Father to fetch him home (the scenes should give scope for the children's

imagination in the words and behaviour of the two boys and the other characters).

*Better Days*
The teacher explains that Louis makes more friends; one who has the bed next to his becomes a life-long friend, Gabriel Gunthler. Another, Joseph, sixteen years old, is specially helpful. They teach him all manner of things of vital importance to a blind person trying to 'feel' and 'listen' his way to greater freedom of life. He learns to run and laugh and jump – and he enters the world of music. But there remains the one great disappointment. As he said at that time to his good friend the Curé, 'Without books, real books – we blind can never learn.' In fact, even at the Institute there were only a handful of books and leaflets, for understandable reasons.

*The New Alphabet*[1]
(a) It will be necessary to explain the difficulty Louis was up against, in common with all other blind people, a difficulty he was to solve at the age of fifteen. It is clearly explained in the book of reference[12] and the children can discover it for themselves. Large cut out letters are needed, and the children close their eyes, and try to 'read' a few sentences. (Even an improvement on the 'letter' method, when a 'sign' was used proved hardly more useful.)
(b) An exciting event in the life of the Institute can be told by the teacher, when its founder, Valentin Huay, is given a Celebration Party – and dramatized.[13]

Finally, an explanation of the 'raised dot' method discovered by Louis Braille must be given, with a dramatized scene to follow.[14] It is October 1824. After years of search, Louis finds the way.

## Speech corrections
In general, fluency, vigour and clarity of meaning are more important than correctness. Remember too that it does not matter in class drama if several children speak at once, or even, at the beginning, if they cannot be heard. (Reasons for improving audibility can be given in the drama, e.g. because of a distant or deaf character.) However, errors of grammar and pronunciation and the faults of monotony and lack of sound clarity

do need correcting. Avoid giving corrections during creative work and preferably not in front of other children. Also, consider the locality.

> Speech is defective when it deviates so far from the speech of other people that it calls attention to itself, interferes with communications, or causes its possessor to be maladjusted.[15]

Speech defects can be caused by psychological or physical troubles. The area school psychologist, speech therapist and school medical officer should be consulted. In class, try to give the child concerned as much calm security and lack of embarrassment as possible. Listen to him patiently. There should be plenty of opportunities for him to join in group speaking and to give answers to questions needing only a brief response.

Defects of habit, again if serious, can be referred to the speech therapist. However, if he has learnt to recognize errors and understands what is wrong and why, aiming to eliminate carelessness rather than dialect, the teacher can help with minor difficulties.

Briefly some errors to look out for are:

| | |
|---|---|
| TH instead of S, e.g. | ('yeth') |
| F instead of TH | ('Frow') |
| V instead of TH | ('Muvver') |
| W instead of R | ('wubber') |
| Dropped L | (Mi(l)k) |
| ,, H | ((h)ungry) |
| ,, G | (gettin(g)) |
| ,, T | (be(tt)er) |
| Added K | (anythink) |

*Useful Exercises*

It is hoped that there will be many opportunities for vocal acrobatics in the drama situation (see section on sound and elsewhere in book). Articulation, enunciation and expressive use of the voice should improve through this. However, if articulation and enunciation are faulty and pace and volume are markedly lacking in variety, specific exercises can be practised. Children can also invent their own, and use jibberish.

e.g. Humming and M/N/NG; LILLY/LALLY; repeated
OO/EE; KICKER/GAGGER; repeated
TICKER/TACKER/DIGGER/DOGGER (start slow – increase speed)

*Tongue Twisters*

e.g. A twister of twists once twisted a twist. The twist that he twisted was a three twisted twist. If in twisting the twist, one twist should untwist the twist that he twisted would be a two twisted twist.

Q: Is it a thin fish or a thick fish?
A: It's a thin fish with a thick fin.

Statement: There once was a selfish shellfish
Who lived by the salt seashore
Q: Why was the shellfish selfish?
A: Because he stayed on the shore by himself.

Children enjoy making up their own. It is fun trying them like a round, in groups, entering in canon. Vary speeds and volumes.

*Some common mispronunciations*

| *Correct* | *Incorrect* |
|---|---|
| opposit | oppos*ite* |
| sandwich | *san*wich |
| gardn | gard*en* |
| cu(p)bd | cupbo*ar*d |
| February | Febr*y* |
| tune | *choon* |
| length | le*n*th |
| parcl | parc*e*l |
| duke | *j*uke |
| drawing | dra*wr*ing |
| facts | fa*x* |
| kitchen | kitch*ing* |
| cunstable | c*o*nstable |
| umbrella | umb*er*ella |
| multiply | m*o*ltiply |
| fifth | fi*th* |
| window | win*der* |
| clothes | cl*os* |
| ghosts | gho*ss* |

## The problem of noise

We must expect a certain amount of noise to occur during drama sessions. Children must be encouraged to speak freely and to use vocal and instrumental sound. However, the drama teacher can make sure that noise does not remain at a constant high level and have suitable consideration for other teachers. He can see that doors are kept shut and place the amplifier, if in use, intelligently. Also, chairs, rostra and other objects can be lifted not dragged. Order within the class should be carefully maintained on entering and leaving the hall.

## Scripted plays

As indicated in the Introduction, in general teachers are advised not to undertake scripted plays in the Primary School. One objection to their use lies in the obstacle the printed word places in the way of drama experience. As children struggle to remember or read, vitality, spontaneity and all sense of the flow of action, of character, of feeling, of drama, is lost.

To quote the Plowden Report, 'Some of our witnesses regarded drama as an integral part of English. Yet drama embraces movement, gesture and mime. And these primitive features of drama should be emphasized with young children especially since plays written for them are usually of indifferent quality and do little to extend or clarify their experience.'[16] If you use scripted plays or extracts from them occasionally with older children (as suggested in the topic on p. 152) make sure the content is suitable and the literary quality high. Also try to keep it lively and interesting; employ creative work techniques building from within the action rather than imposing inflection, gestures and moves. Folk plays such as The Mummers' play *St. George and the Dragon* are suitable for first experience of scripted plays, especially if they demand improvised sections and for lively action opportunities.

## Performances by the children

> Today is the great day for the play and me. For although I have had a speaking part in a play I have never done one in front of an audience. The play has been successful both times but this time must be the best.
>
> (Joan, aged 9)

The end-product of drama in the Primary School should be the experience of it, the process rather than a performance to an audience.

'Though some primary school children enjoy having an audience of other children or their parents, formal presentation of plays on a stage is usually out of place.' (Plowden Report). Communication with an audience in the adult theatre sense cannot be possible with children of this age. Giving a performance usually means that techniques are imposed on the children before they are ready for them and so often the audience has not sufficient understanding or control to behave appropriately. However, sometimes it is necessary to offer a programme of work to parents. In this case teachers should keep the occasion as informal and as like ordinary class work as possible without worrying the children with either long drilling rehearsals or last-minute instructions. If possible avoid emphasis on solo work. Work with puppets can be shown satisfactorily sometimes.

Sometimes work is shown to another class, or the head teacher, and this is one way of drawing a piece of work to a close. This kind of sharing of experience depends largely on the attitude of the teachers concerned and whether their aims and interests are in accord.

Plays at religious festivals, Christmas, Easter, Harvest, are often demanded in school, and if intelligently introduced to the children taking part, and presented carefully, can be successful.

Elaborate sets should be avoided unless made by the children, and lighting, if used at all with the eleven to thirteen age group, used simply to create atmosphere, to focus on/or create locales and to link one scene with the next. If possible, a simple dimmer board should be used adjacent to the action on the floor of the hall. Children can learn to use this.

## Nativity plays

Here are four alternative ideas for teachers who are faced with the task of presenting a Nativity play at Christmas. Allow the children to invent, create, select as much of all this for themselves as possible. Avoid acting as a 'producer' in the adult theatre sense.

1. *Static tableaux and simple processions*, based on pre-sixteenth-century pictures such as postcard reproductions available at the British Museum, London. Accompanying carols and Christmas music performed by different groups/classes. An atmosphere of reverence is the aim which simple lighting/dimness/darkness contrast can aid, fading in and out on the tableaux in turn. (Light coming from the crib itself makes an interest-

ing focus. See *Adoration of the Shepherds* by Gerard Van Honthorst.) The tableaux could move into their positions on rostra or secure tables tied together, around the sides of half the hall, with at least six feet between each. If different levels can be obtained, so much the better. That the children should move into their positions is important if posed, lifeless groups are to be avoided. The success of this idea depends on the absorption and concentration of the participants who should hold the stillness without stiffness and with life. Success also depends on the grouping and colours worn, on the enthusiasm, confidence and good standard of the choral and instrumental work.

Some teachers will prefer to base the narrative on Bible readings, others may like to include readings from Christmas poems, or extracts from St. Bonaventura's *Life of Jesus*[17]. Whatever is chosen, care should be taken in selecting from the children who volunteer for the task, those who are not nervous, can read audibly and with understanding. Sometimes it is better to have a small group of children reading in unison, taking care to avoid a meaningless sing-song repetition of the verses based on a half-hearted imitation of the teacher.

Although the line of the costume could be based on a pre-sixteenth-century period selected by the teacher, this does not mean elaborate or expensive effects are to be aimed at. Indeed, effective use can be made of well-ironed lengths of easily draped material in plain colours, approximately one yard wide. A little gold rope/braid and pieces of fur are useful to add to Kings' costumes (see Gerard David, *The Adoration of the Kings*, c.1480) and a search should be made for authentic-looking shepherds/kings gifts. Attention should be given to appropriate contrasts of texture: e.g. one shepherd might wear a piece of sheepskin, one sacking; one king might wear a heavily embossed piece of brocade as a cloak, for another a velvet curtain might be found, etc.

*Angels.* Care should be taken with footwear avoiding plimsols or noisy everyday shoes. Angels and some shepherds can be bare-foot but others should if possible have slippers of plain felt or of similar material in Medieval/Tudor style. Angels can often need wings: large ones and with some attempt at feathers, in curled paper for instance. Halos sometimes too, preferably of wire and rising above the head, held by wire at the back. Effective use can be made of backings for the scenes, for example wicker fencing or rough wood for the stable. If it is not possible to make an ox and ass head from papiermâché on a wire base or from a clay mould, the heads can be painted life-size on to pieces of cloth and either held by the children medieval style, or fastened to the backing material. (See British Museum postcard reproduction of the Nativity ADD M5 17868 f 16 b for animal heads at the crib.)

2. *Tableaux with additional movement.* Here, more interesting use could be made of the entries, for example, in one scene Joseph and Mary would be in position, looking out down the hall, and the three shepherds would approach from the far end of the hall – perhaps the youngest first, eager to arrive, and another one helping the old man of the group. Perhaps they pause half-way almost wondering if they are going in the right direction. Or perhaps the angels begin to sing again and they pause, awestruck, before resuming their journey. Here, in addition to points made above, success depends on involvement and ability in movement. It is usually more satisfactory if the children have been able to use their own ideas for the journeys rather than imitate the teacher.

3. *The Nativity play as a movement drama with speech and music.* This is a more ambitious undertaking and cannot be attempted happily unless the children have already had experience of movement and drama. The principles to follow concerning content are those described for *The Great Stone Fire Eater*[18]. Use ideas mentioned in methods 1 and 2 above but give additional attention to finding opportunities for movement and speech expression, springing naturally from the story. Both for narrative content and movement ideas teachers can make use of extracts from the medieval mystery plays, for instance the Spicers' play of Annunciation, The Tile Thatchers' play of the Nativity, the Chandlers' Play of the Shepherds, the Goldsmiths' play of the Kings from the York mystery cycle; the Wakefield Second Shepherd's play, and/or the Coventry Nativity play of the Company of Shearmen and Tailors. Again, use can be made of the Bible narrative and also Christmas poems.

It is best to follow the conventions of early English religious drama, and enact the play in the main body of the hall, rather than on a proscenium stage, using rostrum blocks and journeys between them. The audience/congregation can sit all round the action, or on three sides, or in avenue formation with the action down the middle, as well as on the stage, if there is one.

The main movement event to make use of, is the procession. This can be treated as a regular or irregular pattern. As many children as possible should take part. Not only are groups of shepherds, and kings required, but also groups of country folk can come from far and wide and converge round the Holy Family. See *Adoration of the Magi*, Filippino Lippi. They could provide a chorus, as in the play by Christopher Fry, *The Boy with a Cart.*[19] Some could carry lanterns, effective in darkness.

4. *The Nativity play performed by rod and/or shadow puppets.* Here the advantage is that we can avoid the embarrassment and sentimentality, also the tension of some children and showing off of others, sometimes induced by children's performances. A large screen, made from very thin sheeting or firm gauze, is required with light source behind it. This needs to measure at least eight feet from side to side and four feet from top to bottom. (The size partly depends on (a) the number of children taking part (b) the size of the audience/congregation.) There has to be sufficient room behind the screen for the participants, the puppets must be large enough to be effective from the back of the audience, a king to stand at least one foot high, for instance. The screen has to be raised so that the audience can see and to allow room for the children below the line of vision. (The puppets are operated from below and behind the screen and held up against it.) Interesting effects can be obtained with coloured lighting changes and silhouette or filigree cut-outs. The children can make the puppets very simply in one piece of card or with jointed arms, hands and heads. Several figures can be cut from one piece of card for a group effect. Lines of loaded camels with kings, flocks of sheep with shepherds, outlines of other houses near the stable and inn, are just a few of the many ideas that can be tried. Music and words are important component parts of this method. Music again could consist of sung carols and instrumental work. Alternatively, recorded music could be used, such as carols performed by a cathedral choir, or Benjamin Britten's *Ceremony of Carols* (or the twelfth-century music drama *The Play of Herod* realized by Charles Ravier for Ensemble Polyphonique of French National Radio and recorded). If it is decided to use recorded orchestral works, extracts from pieces such as the following could be used:

| *Scene* | *Suggested Music* |
| --- | --- |
| Introduction: The darkness of the World | from Holst, *The Planets*, 'Saturn' |
| The Annunciation | from R. Vaughan Williams, *Variations on a theme of Thomas Tallis* and *Lark ascending* for violin and orchestra |
| The people go to be taxed | either percussion recorded by the children or an extract from a currently available percussion record could be used |
| Bethlehem | from R. Vaughan Williams, *Job* |
| The Nativity | from *Lark ascending* for Violin and orchestra and *Variations on a theme of Thomas Tallis* |
| The Kings and Herod | from Holst, *The Planets*/'Jupiter' from Ravel, *Mother Goose Suite*, 'Prince of the Pagodas' |
| The Shepherds | from arrangement of music by Bach, *Wise Virgins Ballet Suite*, Bach *Sheep May Safely Graze*, *Ah How Ephemeral are thy dwellings* |
| At the Stable | from R. Vaughan Williams, *Variations on a theme of Thomas Tallis* |
| Conclusion: Vision of St. John | from R. Vaughan Williams, *Variations on a theme of Thomas Tallis* |

Words could be taken from the Bible, from the medieval plays suggested above, from modern and medieval Christmas poems and carols found in most good school anthologies and carol books.

5. *Christmas customs and folklore*. There are interesting customs and legends from all over the world which can be used as a basis for drama at Christmas time. For example, consider the Mexican Festival of Posedas or the legend of old Befana from Italy. For futher suggestions see *Christmas Customs and Folklore*,[20] and *Christmas*.[28]

## Puppets

Work with puppets can develop dramatic sense and can combine use of craft, speech, movement, and sound, with observation of human beings and animals. This work can also bring the pleasure of participation to children who otherwise do not have sufficient confidence to attempt other dramatic work.

There are several kinds of puppets, some more quickly made than others. In general, the younger children need quicker results than the older ones, and with Infants the using of the puppet is more important than the making.

The teacher can introduce the idea of puppet making and using by referring to their use on TV, or by bringing one in to show the children, allowing them to handle it. He may also tell a story using the puppet, or especially in the case of Infants, sing a song with the puppet's assistance. It is important not to force group work at too early a stage: some children usually prefer to remain alone with their puppet to whom they become very attached. It is also important not to force speech flow with the puppet: with the youngest children there may be few words, in which case the teacher can assist as narrator.

Briefly, glove puppets of clean old socks or paper bags tied round the wrist or with simple heads of potato, pegs, or matchboxes are quickest to make. Material stuffed with rags also makes a fairly simple head, with sewn face using buttons and oddments including string hair, etc. Eight to nine-year-olds can make papiermâché heads quite easily. Teachers are advised to consult the book list for further assistance with puppets.[21–25] The book *Skills in the Junior School*[26] gives clear directions on puppet making for children to follow.

Children enjoy making their puppet behave in various ways and situations. Practical skills to practise in handling the puppet include turning, shaking and nodding the head, clapping hands, rubbing head, eating, carrying something, knocking, polishing, scrubbing, waving one arm, pushing, dancing.

Glove puppets lend themselves to vivid, colourful slapstick drama, adventures and characters and direct address to the audience.

Marionettes, or string puppets are in general more suitable for the older children, though younger ones can make and use the simpler varieties. They lend themselves to human parody, acrobatic, dance and flying movement, also animals.

Rod and shadow puppets can be made by children from infants upwards, and older children become interested in the use of these in Eastern countries, and the beautiful effects which can be obtained. They lend themselves to dignified, simple expressive narrative (see section on Nativity Plays). A theatre structure of some kind is obviously essential for these puppets, and although not essential for glove puppets it adds considerably to the work, especially with the older children. The defined limits of the edges of the puppet stage opening are an interesting challenge for creation of place, atmosphere and mood. A theatre is easily improvised behind a box or table, and more elaborate theatres can be made by using easels, curtains, pieces of cardboard, wood. Making their own puppet theatre has been achieved by children of seven from simple directions, see Lilian Hollamby, *Young Children Living and Learning*.[27]

## Performances for the children

At the Primary school stage it is better to have a theatre group visit the school than to take the children to a theatre. The plays performed to children should have been written with the age group in mind. Opportunity for natural audience participation which may even alter the course of the action, is a good ingredient. However, since the children need to be allowed to enjoy the act of seeing, audience participation should not dominate the event. Themes and plots should be similar to those that children use in their playmaking. The British Children's Theatre Association can give further information.

BOOK REFERENCES

1. Muriel Mandell and Robert E. Wood, *Make Your Own Musical Instruments*, Sterling Publishing Co., New York
2. Raymond Williams, *The Long Revolution*, Chatto and Windus
3. M. M. Lewis, *Language, Thought and Personality in Infancy and Childhood*, Harrap
4. *Report on Primary Schools*, H.M.S.O.
5. Professor F. J. Schonell, *The Listener*, 13 October 1944
6. *Growth and Play*, B.B.C. Publication
7. Aldous Huxley, *Words and their Meanings*
8. Oscar Turnhill, 'Harold Williamson' in 'Interview', *Sunday Times*, 29 December 1968
9. T. S. Eliot, *The Use of Poetry and the Use of Criticism*, Faber and Faber
10. G. Webster, *Journey into Light*, World's Work, Hawthorn Books

11. *Ibid*, Chapters 2, 3 and 4
12. *Ibid*, Chapters 5, 6 and 7
13. *Ibid*, pp. 65–6
14. *Ibid*, Chapter 6
15. C. Van Riper, *Speech Correction*, Constable
16. *The Plowden Report*, H.M.S.O.
17. St. Bonaventura, *Life of Jesus* (tr. from Latin by Edward Yates), Coghlan, 1773
18. 'The Great Stone Fire Eater' in *Folk Tales of All Nations*, ed. F. H. Lee, Harrap 1931
19. Christopher Fry, *The Boy with a Cart*, Frederick Muller Ltd.
20. *Christmas Customs and Folklore*, Discovery Guide Series, Shire Publications
21. W. D. Nicol, *Puppetry*, Oxford University Press
22. Lois H. Pratt, *The Puppet Do it Yourself Book*, Stanley Paul
23. Stuart and Patricia Robinson, *Exploring Puppetry*, Mills and Boon
24. Margaret Beresford, *How to make puppets and teach puppetry*, Mills and Boon
25. Helen Binyon, *Puppetry Today*, Studio Vista
26. Beryl Ash and Barbara Rapaport, *Skills in the Junior School*, Methuen 1960
27. Lilian Hollamby, *Young Children Living and Learning*, Longmans, 1962
28. William Sansom, *Christmas*, Weidenfeld and Nicolson.

# Chapter 7: The Third Stage

This chapter shows how drama can be the main focus in project work or contribute to centre of interest activity which aims to develop children's understanding of other subjects or aspects of life.

Only a limited number of starting points can be presented here. However, these have been chosen to indicate the wide range of possibilities and include environment, Bible story, legend, exploration, geography, history, literature, science, and topical event. Concerning the use of these starting points, the following comments from *The Times* are relevant:

> Our puritanical distaste for the art of dramatization seems to be a mistake. What matters is not possible damage to a novel – the novel remains a valid work, no matter what is done on the stage – but the quality of theatrical excitement and vivid drama which can be quarried from it.[1]

Sometimes topics will be initiated by the children, sometimes by the teacher, based on the agreed interests and needs of the children. It is necessary to keep a balance between teacher-initiated projects and spontaneous class-initiated ones. However, the teacher has to plan ahead if films, filmstrips, visits, information, local library assistance, etc. are required. Indeed, well thought out plans are needed to make this approach effective. Although a certain amount of detailed planning is presented in these notes, it cannot be too strongly emphasized that the intention is to spark off ideas in the reader rather than to give directions.

## CENTRES OF INTEREST

My town
Your nearest city
Characters and themes from history
Floods
A Korean folktale

Explorers
Marco Polo
Columbus
Indians
Introducing Mary Kingsley
Introducing Charles Sturt
Men of Everest 1953
Beowulf
Energy
Ideas from the sky
A topical event

## MY TOWN

A school often seems to be an enclosed world, but in reality, influences are streaming in continuously from outside. Moreover that outside world of the school's environment is alive, and therefore has a past embedded in its active present – and is unique in character. It is only necessary to mention a few localities to emphasize this last point:

Tonypandy in a Welsh mining valley
Dover on the Straits
Norwich amidst East Anglian farmland
A Devon village
A Glasgow district
A London Borough

Exploration by the children of their town will soon reveal, not only its individual character, intimately related to its own geographical setting, but also those powerful outside forces which have impinged on its life and continue to do so.

Since man in his environment has been suggested in this handbook to be the basis of drama work, 'My Town' has an important place in the syllabus.

Both for children whose families belong to the area, and for those from other places, other lands, an introduction to their local town can be of vital interest and value. Sometimes a teacher may wish to take one or two aspects only; at the other end of the scale, say once in five or ten years, a school, or group of schools, may plan a Pageant of the town's history.

## Sources of Information

(a) Local libraries (for the public, for teachers, and for school children) are usually the main sources.
(b) For special subjects, local societies, local experts may be of the greatest help.
(c) Local newspapers, often kept over long periods, can be of fascinating interest if the teacher is searching for particular material.

## Starting Points

(a) The signs of history, past and recent, are not only to be found in books, but on the doorstep and sometimes may serve well as starting points. For example: the name of the School itself, or of a road where a child lives, the old log-books hidden away in a Head teacher's drawer, an alleyway, an old Tudor house, a very winding road, a statue, a local power station, a new block of flats. . . .
(b) A well prepared visit to a local museum, a topical event in the town, a talk by an invited guest.

Instead of giving general ideas, a particular area has been chosen to illustrate possibilities. It is the London Borough of Waltham Forest, which in 1965 was formed by the union of three boroughs, Leyton, Walthamstow and Chingford, previously in the County of Essex. (It is fully recognized that the approach will vary according to the nature of the particular area studied.)

The following suggestions are given with these points in mind:

1. The continuing importance through all the years of the basic facts in the situation of the area:
   Waltham Forest is bounded on the east by forest land, on the west by the broad low-lying Lea Valley with its marshlands – beyond which is London.
2. The local people mentioned as stimuli for playmaking have been selected mainly because they are likely to be of interest to any reader. (Of course local personalities chosen in environment studies should not normally be limited to well-known men and women.)
3. Obviously the age of the children is considered in the selection of material used.

A map must be the beginning, showing the natural features as they were long ago with the Great Forest of Essex stretching east and north, the Lea Valley, low and marshy, parallel with it, and the famous capital beyond, always a fascination to Essex people who are yet quite separate even now, from it.

The children can begin with two roads they all know, Forest Road and Lea Bridge Road. This brings them immediately to the fundamentals, the Forest, a barrier to expansion eastwards for ever, the Lea which must be crossed to reach London, by ferry, bridge – or tunnel. This last word can be used to evoke an idea – which is, to begin with the immediate present, not with the remote past of Roman times. Hence the first dramatic activity could be as follows:

*Opening Day of the new Victoria Line – a Sunday in September, 1968*
It is early in the morning; groups of people have gathered outside the station of the new line (known to all Londoners, now partly constructed, the first of its kind in Britain).

Each group is heard discussing the line in a lively fashion. Mention is made that for the first time the barrier of the Lea Valley is overcome by a tunnel; some refer to the speed of the route; Leytonstone and Chingford are envious. Why should Walthamstow be the favoured one? Some complaints are heard, the trains shake the foundations of the houses, perhaps cracks will appear. (Local newspaper reports and letters concerning these complaints which really were made can be used.) Also, if it can be arranged, perhaps with the help of a student on teaching practice in the school, verbatim reports or even on-the-spot tape recordings could be attempted by the children, of local people affected in some definite way, by the new line. These reports and recordings could be used for background information, or could contribute to a radio or TV play, or could be used as background sound for a movement scene. Recordings of street sounds could also be made.

Another possible scene:

*Queen Victoria is coming!*
It is 1892. Townsfolk or a class in a local school hear the news. The Queen is coming to celebrate the decision to keep Epping Forest for the interest and delight of Londoners 'for ever'. (Again authentic details of the event can be obtained from local papers of the time.) Entertainments are prepared.

Now perhaps the children are ready to find out about the past: such as the following:

*Facts known in early history*

(a) A Roman road was built from London running through the southern part of the area.
(b) Boadicea's armies must have used it to reach London victoriously, but also to retreat along it to the Forest in utter defeat.
(c) The Saxons came when the Romans left, and founded Ley-tun, Wilcumestou and Chingford.

A scene arising from this might be:

*'Shall we settle here?'*
A group of Saxon families have come from the Forest and are on a stretch of riding land sloping down westwards to the marshes of a river valley: they have been here for a few days.

In their talk together the situation can be revealed: for example a boy returns from the Forest, excited and rather frightened. He has seen deer, but also a wolf. A man and woman bring wood from the Forest for a fire. They talk about food; rabbits are mentioned, a child finds luscious blackberries. They realize the land is suitable for farming – they decide to settle there. Finally, they all stand and look west across the river wondering what lies there. Hidden away is, of course, Londinium.

It is now possible to give only the briefest references to scenes which will reflect either the continuing effect of the setting, or the historic currents of the time entering the life of these Forest villages as they slowly grow towards towns.

For example:

*King Alfred plans to foil a group of Danes* (based on the authentic story: the enemy sailed up the Lea from the Thames)
The King is discussing with local people his plan. It is to drain away enough water to make it impossible for the ships to return. They cut channels to draw off water.
or:

*'News from Hastings 1066'*
Two men report the tragic defeat and death of Harold, who had

recently passed through, from Waltham Abbey, gathering support. He held a manor in Ley-tun. Agitated talk and grief is shown with fear for the future.
or:

*The Domesday men make their records*
This scene reveals the immediate effect of the Norman Conquest. One local Saxon lord of the manor retains his rights because he gives allegiance to Duke William. The others are replaced by Normans. The farming nature of the land is commented on.

## Local people as stimulus for playmaking

'*Roger Ascham at Chelsea Palace*' (a local school bears his name)
The famous tutor of Lady Jane Grey, Prince Edward and Elizabeth lived in Salisbury Hall in the locality.

*Sir George Monoux*, who helped in Bristol, to equip the 'Matthew' which took John Cabot in 1497 to Newfoundland. He founded the local Grammar School.

*Sir Thomas Roe*
His family was typical of others in the locality, who had important City connections, but resided in these villages near the Forest. He was of course an Elizabethan adventurer, later an Ambassador and helped to establish the East India Company.

*Rev. Samuel Slater*
He represents another kind of adventurer. He was one of the 2,000 clergy of the Church of England who resisted the 'Act of Conformity' of 1662, accordingly had to leave the parish church. He founded a 'Dissenters' meeting place' later. (In one scene he could be in hiding in a friend's house, discussing with a group of friends the dangers of his situation and his ideas about the Act.)

*Dick Turpin* (Born 1705)
The Forest of course attracted this rogue. A local Inn was his hide-out, with underground rooms. The hazards of travel on horseback and by coach will be reflected in the scene.

*Tom Hood*, whose humorous poem, 'The Epping Hunt' about a Cockney sportsman in Epping Forest can be used to introduce the group of Quakers who formed quite a colony locally in his day. Their meeting house was next to Tom Hood's home. (It has just been rebuilt in modern style.) The poem could be used as the basis of a scene.

*Ebenezer Cogan*
Unitarian Minister and founder of a local school which admitted boys not allowed for political or religious reasons to attend others. Benjamin Disraeli was a pupil. The well-known scene which led to Disraeli's expulsion can be enacted.

*William Morris*
Artist, craftsman, socialist, poet, and lover of Epping Forest from childhood days. His words 'Fellowship is Life' were chosen by Walthamstow as the town motto, and now are illustrated on the Waltham Forest coat of arms.

Appropriately enough, the new Victoria Line station at Walthamstow has as its sign a panel showing a design of his, with plants and flowers such as he might have seen in the Forest; he fought with others to preserve its beauty for the people to enjoy 'for ever'.

Finally, various scenes are possible arising from 'The Coming of the Railway' (L.N.E.R.), and other aspects of local life, such as the street markets.

Also, since the last war, Waltham Forest has made links with Hamburg and St. Mandé on the outskirts of Paris. This fact might lead to other scenes.

## YOUR NEAREST CITY

Your nearest city could provide source material for drama. As an example, London:

1. *London in Early Times*
The first settlers, the coming of the Romans, Roman London, everyday life in Roman London, the departure of the Romans, the Saxons and the Vikings.

2. *London During the Middle Ages*
The Norman Conquest, the Tower of London, churches and monas-

teries, how London was governed, the city companies or guilds, markets and fairs, trade with other lands, pilgrimages, houses and homes, transport and pastimes.

3. *London Under the Tudors*
Overcrowding: slums and new suburbs, London in the time of Henry VIII, the new wealth in Tudor London, industries and crafts, Tudor streets and houses, entertainments and the theatre.

4. *London Under the Stuarts*
The growing population, Inigo Jones, the Civil War, the Great Plague, the Great Fire, London after the fire, fashionable London life in Stuart times, Restoration playhouses.

5. *London in Georgian Times*
The beginning of the Empire, the new bridges, poverty and crime, hospitals and medicine for the poor, trade and dock-building in the Port of London, wealth and commerce, trades and industries, shops and streets, visitors and travellers, regency society, entertainments.

6. *London in the Reign of Queen Victoria.*
Transport including the coming of the railways; the growth of the slums, the relief of the poor, the Great Exhibition, banking and stock-broking, markets and shops, factories and workers, the unemployed, Victorian houses and homes, museums, e.g. Madame Tussauds, society life, entertainments and the theatre, leisure and crime.

7. *Modern London*
The Port of London, London's industries, city and West End offices, modern streets, homes in central London, new plans for the city, some sights and ceremonies, London's museums.

SELECTED BOOK LIST

*London's River*, Eric de Mare. Bodley Head.
*London: from the earliest times to the present day*, John Hayes. A. and C. Black.
*The Thames: London's River*, Noel Streatfield (a story for children). Frederick Muller.
*Greater London*, Christopher Trent. Phoenix House.

*The Survey of London*, John Stow (about Elizabethan London). J. M. Dent.
*A Book of London Yesterdays*, Frederick Willis. Phoenix House,
*The B. P. Book of Festivals and Events in Britain*, Christopher Trent. Phoenix House. (This book describes 250 events from around Britain including London.)

## CHARACTERS AND THEMES FROM HISTORY

Events of 1066
Forest game laws and punishments: hunting
Trial by ordeal and combat. Hue and cry. Outlaws
The feudal system
Pilgrimages and Fairs
Saxon resistance to the Normans
Becket
Wat Tyler and the peasants' revolt
The Burghers of Calais
Chaucer – extracts from *Canterbury Tales*
Famous sailors of Tudor England: Raleigh, Frobisher, Hudson, Drake, Grenville, Gilbert Hawkins
Guy Fawkes
Mayflower Pilgrims
John Bunyan
Fire of London
Plague

Use the original source books, diaries, autobiographies wherever possible. (The Jackdaw series published by Jonathan Cape is very helpful.) Details of costume, social life, music, communications, transport, theatre, literature, inventions and famous people of the time can provide drama material. A useful example of how a historical event can be treated dramatically is *Journal 1665*.[2]

## FLOODS

*The Flood*, from Genesis VI, VII, VIII and IX (Authorized version, other versions to be used if preferred). Genesis VI 5–8, 11, 13–14, 17–18. VII 17, 23. VIII from 1–5, 6–20. IX from 13.

The dramatic activity falls naturally into nine scenes:

(a) Evidence of evil, violence and corruption amongst men.
(b) Voice of God (this could be a voice or voices or imagined, with instead a sound such as deep-sounding gong or drum roll).
(c) Emergence of Noah and family; God speaks to Noah.
(d) The building of the ark. Reactions from other people: mockery, violence, regret.
(e) The rains and floods come: reactions of panic/drowning; the group on the ark are secure and safe.
(f) The ark floats and moves on a silent vastness of water.
(g) The wind and the cessation of rain and flood. The ark touches ground. The raven and dove are sent out. The dove returns with olive leaf and goes again.
(h) God speaks and all leave the ark; reactions to being on the ground after about a year in the ark.
(i) The building of the altar and sacrifice. God's blessing and rainbow.

Also see *The Epic Story of Giglamesh* (available in Penguin classic publications) for another version of the flood story, extracts of which could be used for dramatization; and *Noyes Fludde* from the medieval Chester cycle of Mystery plays. Extracts from this play could be used by the eleven to thirteen-year-old age group, or as background narrative for the younger children. Indications of character such as Noah's wife's reluctance to get into the ark, and the subsequent arguments are worth noting as possible ideas for improvisation, also the splendid speech of the Gossip:

The flood comes in full fleeting fast
On every side it broadens in haste;
For fear of drowning I am aghaste:
Good gossip, let me come in!
Or let us drink ere we depart
For often times we have done so!
For at a time thou drinkst a quart,
And so will I, ere that I go.

Teachers may also like to make use of Benjamin Britten's opera version of this play, or ideas from it, such as the use of struck tea cups as one of the sources of sound for the rain.

No mention has been made of the animals: the teacher and class can do as much or as little with these in movement and costume as they wish, from simple stylized representation to more realistic using masks, gloved paws and swishing tails. The children can choose which animals they want to include and should be given the opportunity of finding out about the existence of as many different animals, birds, insects, reptiles as they can. Simple stylized representation can even be large banner-pictures of the animal being carried along (as some authorities quote as medieval practice). If representation in movement is chosen as the method, the teacher must make sure that the children's choice of animal/bird/insect/reptile is made bearing potential movement content in mind. The children should be encouraged to observe animals, etc., to see how they move and interesting movement is then more likely to result.

## The North Sea Floods of 1953

The starting point can be the famous Dutch story of the boy on the dyke, which can be dramatized. The children should be introduced to the reality of the 1953 Floods which affected the coastlands of Holland and of England from the Humber to the Thames. A map of the North Sea is essential, showing low-lying coastal regions where the sea area narrows towards the Straits of Dover.

*Why these terrible floods?*
The following notes suggest how the children can be prepared to find the answer themselves.

*Class discussion* (Appropriate of course to age of children)
(a) Daily weather reports. The children have been encouraged to listen to these for a week or two.
(b) Tides. Possible reasons for specially high tides are considered. (Readers may remember that the floods were caused by exceptionally powerful north winds at the high tide period driving the water towards the bottle-neck at the narrow Straits of Dover.)

*BBC News Report on the growing danger*
(Authentic details of reports coming in from coastal towns of Britain and from Holland can be obtained by the teacher from *The Great Tide*.[3]) The suggestion made here is that, using a large map, the children can act as radio reporters in London and at the places marked on the

map, the build-up of the disastrous conditions on the Dutch coast and the opposite English coast can be demonstrated. The teacher will tell the children of the northerly gales of exceptional violence, reported first from northern coast towns and ships in distress in mid-North Sea; then how news comes from towns further south, of continued gales, rising tide, mounting danger to low-lying areas. The children can then prepare their reports from their own station. The BBC 'man' broadcasts a summary of news received during the preceding twelve hours. He pauses now and then for the voice of the 'reporters' to be heard, beginning of course with the early news from the north. In the later news, the growing threat to the Dutch people, and to certain towns like Mablethorpe is revealed. Mention is then made of emergency measures being taken. Class discussion and improvization can alternate. The teacher can discuss the areas in greatest danger and what it will mean for people, animals, buildings. The danger of Holland with its excellent farmland behind the dykes, at a level lower than the sea can be shown.

*Scene: On Canvey Island as the flood rises*
As usual, class discussion is needed first.

*Suggestions*

(a) The terrible emergency is made clear by groups of people and individuals arriving, from the same direction, some carrying goods of all kinds. Old people stumble along, a woman is sobbing and collapses. She tells of disasters seen, animals drowned. . . .

(b) An Emergency Committee on the Island is outlining plans. The leader speaks of Army and Navy men coming to help, to pile up sandbags on the coast, of police help in taking away old people and children, WVS emergency relief centres, rescue operations by boat.

Groups of children can dramatize these activities. This can be done in various ways. Here are suggestions:

(i) Groups of soldiers are doing the motions of moving and piling up sandbags. They work desperately, with hardly breath to speak, and almost drop from exhaustion.

(ii) A policeman enters quickly, finds a child wandering and frightened, clutching a small dog. Two women run in, dishevelled. They tell their story. The policeman takes them to car.

(iii) An improvised relief centre. Two women in charge talk rapidly, looking anxiously in one direction. They speak of increasing danger to the island as floods are said to be advancing from the east; news of deaths has been heard.

(iv) An imaginary loudspeaker van arrives as women are talking. They listen as the announcer says the island is to be evacuated, boats are coming to rescue the inhabitants. Everyone is told to leave at once. Directions are given. The announcer's voice is heard again further off. People come hurrying along.

*Scene: Children on the Church Tower*

This suggestion is based on an actual event in Holland during the disastrous floods, which a Dutch writer, Jan de Hartog, made the basis of a story. (It was broadcast in Britain as a serial later, and an extract from it is included in the *Oxford Book of Stories for Juniors* by J. Britton.[4] The title is 'The Little Ark'.)

*Story incidents which can be given to the children on which they base their drama* (this story is not identical with the one mentioned above).

The scene is a village on the Dutch coast where dykes protect the land, so low that it is actually below sea level. There is a church with a belfry tower. The pastor and his wife are accustomed to allow the children to go up the belfry and play there. One Sunday they ring the bell, as the pastor cannot climb the stairs. On the day when the floods are rising and a terrible gale is blowing, he goes through it with four children, a boy of thirteen, a girl of twelve, a boy of eight, and a girl of six, to the tower. The children go up and he returns. Floods begin to invade the village; the children look down from the tower, only to realize they cannot go down. They have some food with them.

Now the class can discuss their dramatized scene. Some suggestions here will indicate possibilities: there can of course be a larger group of children, or several different groups. The elder boy may be active in looking out and noticing the scene, calling the elder girl to look. They may see people in houses at top windows, catch a glimpse of people on the dyke, see animals in danger. . . . The elder girl may try to comfort the younger ones, protect them from the terrible gale, perhaps find some sacking to protect them. Perhaps they will think of the best way to use the food. Night comes, they huddle down. Morning comes, the elder boy looks out first, water is much higher. He catches sight of a boat drifting near the tower. He picks up a rope and disappears; comes back and wakens the others. He has caught hold of the boat from a window at a lower level. They anxiously wonder if they should go away with it.

If the children have been inventing their own plays from incidents such as these and from factual background, it might then be interesting for them to hear the story 'The Little Ark' mentioned above.

### Local floods

If there has been any recent local occurrence of flooding perhaps the children, their family or friends have had first hand experience which can provide a basis for improvisation and playmaking including documentary programmes (radio or TV). And here we can satisfy the primitive/child need for re-enactment of life events – there is an interesting Polynesian drama based on the event of a tidal wave. The children should be encouraged to collect verbatim reports: with the teacher's help perhaps a tape recorder could be used for some of these which can then be incorporated into the programme. These reports, interspersed with music and sound could also provide part of a background sound montage for movement work. Try to hear one of Ewan McColl's radio ballads (e.g. 'Singing the Fishing' available on record – Argo recording) for further help with effects and techniques of this type of documentary work.

## A KOREAN FOLK TALE

Interesting themes for dramas and dance dramas can be found in the culture of different countries or areas. When using stories as a basis for drama, the first questions to ask are, is the story likely to interest the children, to suit and extend their understanding, to stimulate them to dramatic activity, to satisfy their needs?

As previously implied, drama should contain situation, leading to action and/or plot, and atmosphere building, characterization, group work. It should also be of suitable content for classroom or larger space, should contain opportunities for movement and language (including speech teaching). Other possible adjuncts or integral parts might be art and craft work, music, folk, national or international background.

## Procedure: adaptation and use of the story

Is the language used in telling the story of as good literary quality as possible? Will it encourage language enjoyment and development? The experienced teacher usually tells stories such as this in his own words, but when well written folk-tales are available, he may sometimes prefer to read them to the class. Some changes or explanation of the language may be necessary.

A story as it exists should not simply be retold in action. It is sometimes desirable either to select scenes from the story or to telescope scenes together to achieve a basis suitable for drama experience. Some scenes can be told briefly by a narrator, and some acted. The children themselves will as often as not suggest which scenes they want to try out, and notice should be taken of their suggestions. In fact since at this stage we are not concerned with communicating with or impressing the audience, it is not necessary to stress the arts of production. But the aim of the teacher is to put interesting, worthwhile opportunities for dramatic expression within reach of the children. And since one way in which drama can be made interesting or even exist at all, is in its structure and build-up of anticipation, suspense, climax and interaction of contrasting characters, groups and situations, some suggestions can gradually be given to the older children of the Primary School on these matters. The teacher too will present or tell the story in such a way as to draw attention to this dramatic content. But when the children set to work remember Kipling:

> There are nine and sixty ways of constructing tribal lays
> And every single one of them is right.

One point to consider is the order of the scenes. It is sometimes better for the statement of theme, character and shaping of the drama, including contrast and climax build-up, to alter the story order. The following is an example of a drama particularly stressing action, with speech if desired, developed from a Korean folk tale, *The Great Stone Fire-Eater*.[5]

It is sometimes necessary to add characters. In this story, the Emperor's daughter and her friends were not in the original story but provide a good lyrical contrast to the other courtly characters. Through drama, some characters or aspects of the story can be stressed more than others.

Having studied the needs and interests of the class and chosen the story with these in mind, now consider the content of the story, what possibilities does it afford? Briefly, the situation is this: an Emperor and his people have a problem, fire devils are a constant threat. They come often, and when least expected. What can be done? First outside help (rain dragon) is sought but proves useless. Then the people set to providing their own solution and thus gain release from their terror.

The drama might begin with a representation of life in the Emperor's court, the palace guards enter and courtiers converse with each other. Their characters differ: pompous, flamboyant, flattering, efficient, incompetent and servile. In creating the court there is an opportunity for the children to become 'scenery' as well as people, for instance they could become in groups gates of different natures which open and close in different ways, all suitably named, e.g. the gate of sizzling iron (which venomously slides open and shut) – the children should sense the firm, relentless nature of the iron; the hanging gate, the gate of lotus blossoms – (the children should experience the delicacy of the flowers – perhaps opening successively), the golden gate, the gate of jade. The gates open to allow courtiers through and close immediately after. The most important moment comes when the Emperor arrives with his attendants. Perhaps it is his birthday and the courtiers and his children come to pay their respects. In developing drama there should always be reasons for action, reasons for any journey made.

Having approached and greeted the Emperor in characteristic ways, perhaps in different groups, there might be very brief dance or courtly ritual sequence in his honour, rudely interrupted by the descent of the fire devils. There are to be three visits of the fire devils so it is important to think of these in relation to each other and to the development of the action and climax. The South Wind is an optional character or group, working in conjunction with the fire devils. There are three clear, contrasting movement possibilities for the fire attacks (with various methods of retreat)

(a) Direct
(b) Around
(c) Passing through.

The second possibility can be around the entire courtly group, or around sections of the courtly group who have formed huddled towers in response to the fire threat.

However, before even the fire arrives for the first attack, rumours of its coming can spread, and much activity results: attempts made to collect belongings, to protect the emperor, to reinforce the palace and so on.

There are at least two alternative approaches to the characterization of the Emperor. He could be the strong leader, taking the initiative at times of difficulty, or hesitant, uncertain, relying heavily on his fortune tellers, astrologers and ministers, both scrupulous and otherwise, for advice.

At this point, whichever characterization is chosen, the decision has to be reached by the Emperor with or without advisers, to send for the mist-breathing rain dragon from China. There will be a hiatus during the journeys of the messengers and the dragon, so the court folk can prepare for the dragon's arrival by such activities as making the palace even more splendid, by preparing a feast, by practising dances and acrobatics.

When the dragon (or dragons, if preferred) arrives, with or without dragon keepers, of course he is given a great welcome. He brings a feeling of security and contentment to the court. He is so spoiled, petted and well fed that, with the court, he falls asleep. Effective, enjoyable dragons can be made best by about five or six people, but it is most important for experiments with almost any number to be tried before selection is made. Also, what does the dragon look like? What colours is he? Is he fierce or friendly? What are his idiosyncracies? Is he eccentric in any way? How can all this be shown in movement?

When the fire visits for a second time, the atmosphere, and therefore the action, should become more urgent. The dragon hides and is discovered trembling in a far corner, and banished. Now the people have to think up a solution for themselves. The treatment of this depends largely on how far a consistent style is being aimed at throughout. For instance, if an everyday, not specifically oriental style is being used in gesture and speech, this can continue through this scene as people meet to discuss the problem and invent schemes both wild and practical. However, if a more Eastern flavour has been aimed at and achieved, at this point a series, possibly three 'thinks' can occur in groups of five to seven children, each 'think' being within a phrase of rhythm and movement and consisting of a preparation and arrival in a different group position signifying which area of the universe is being consulted, or the knottiness of the problem. This phrase beaten out on hardsticks might be:

𝅗𝅥 𝅗𝅥 ♩ ♩ ♩ ♫ ♫ ♫ ♩ ‖

After this, one or more representatives from each group could present the results of thinking to the Emperor – and the decision is made to excavate a lake and build a frightening statue of white granite with a grotesque swivelling head. There may be some argument and disagreement about the relative merits of the plans, but if a well constructed drama is being aimed at, with a good pulsing rise to the climax, do not delay too long at this point or give time for over-indulgence in argumentation.

A working action scene follows. The work can be as simple or rhythmically intricate as the age and capabilities of the children permit (see section on movement). The activities here will contrast dynamically with the ensuing silence and stillness of the group as they wait, with backs turned for the arrival of the fire demons. As well as digging and filling the lake with water, it has been found successful for the children to imagine they find and transport the block of stone to do the carving, chiselling, hammering, etc., actions and also to become the statue itself as they make it. The South Wind may take news of the work to the fire devils who mock but are curious to see for themselves. Anyway, the climax of the piece occurs when the fire devils, having sidled round the lake warily, approach the strange blank back of the swivelling statue and suddenly round it turns with the most frightening, grotesque faces and twisted bodies it can manage. At this the fire devils are so terrified they tumble and stagger backwards into the water with a dying hiss. Jubilant, the Emperor and his people celebrate their liberation from the threat with a danced procession.

## Movement

The starting point of this legend leads well to movement experience. So now, some suggestions as to which aspects of movement training can be included.

As with any movement in drama activity, the content can be thought of under the following headings:

A. *Specific Use of the body* – or what moves
B. *Expressive Use of the body* – or how we move
C. *Use of the space* – or where we move
D. *Partner and/or group work* – or with whom we move
E. *Form*

Included within A. *Specific Use of the body* – or what moves, are activities of stepping, leaping, jumping, turning, travelling, in fact different methods of weight transference; gesturing and carriage, or bodily attitude. All these do combine. Also included are actions of holding, gripping, gathering, scattering, opening, closing, twisting, rising, lowering, falling. Differentiation of body areas and parts belong in this section: top/bottom half of the body, left/right side of the body, front back feet, knees, elbows, etc. etc.

Included with B. *Expressive Use of the Body* or how we move is the movement content which brings about characterization and mood in drama. This means using different combinations of movement elements arising from an attitude towards the motion factors.[1]

| *Motion factor* | *Movement element* |
| --- | --- |
| *Weight* | (a) Firm, strong<br>or<br>(b) delicate, gentle |
| *Time* | (a) sudden, urgent<br>or<br>(b) slow, sustained |
| *Space* | (a) direct, straight<br>or<br>(b) round about, flexible |
| *Flow* | (a) unrestrained, free<br>or<br>(b) cautious, bound |

Of course there are many different shadings of these elements and ways of combining them and building sequences.

Generally speaking in lesson preparation it is helpful to analyse the

[1] These suggestions are based on Rudolph Laban's Principles and Practice of Movement.

characters, moods, and hence the movement characteristics, movement ideas and phrases needed in terms of these broadly stated motion factors. However, since it is important that the children work directly from the stimuli of character and mood, and explore and invent their own movement, in the teaching situation 'movement jargon' invented for the teacher, should not be used repetitiously. If it is opportunities for enjoyment of language and extending vocabulary are lost, cliché movement may result and the zest can go out of the drama. The important thing is for the teacher to be aware of and to understand the dramatic movement experience which he wishes to give the children, and here even a simple analysis in movement terms will help him. He will thus be helped to decide what his teaching content should be.

To illustrate what is meant by this, let us take the character of the fire devils from *The Great Stone Fire Eater*.[5]

*Character*: such as, sprightly, attacking, lively, devouring, powerful, destructive, causing fear, awesome.

*Movement ideas or characteristics*: such as, growing, increasing, bursting out, travelling, surrounding, spreading, infiltrating, changing levels.

*Movements* such as

*quick, flickering jumps*
Weight: light
Time: sudden
Space: flexible
Flow: bound

*large surrounding movements*
Weight: strong
Time: sustained
Space: direct
Flow: free

*slashing turn*
Weight: strong
Time: sudden
Space: flexible
Flow: free

*jerky, sharp, biting movements*
Weight: strong
Time: sudden
Space: direct
Flow: bound

Then the teacher can use the ideas and stimulate the children into movement experience and phrasing by what he says such as: 'The fire devils live down in the depths of a volcano, so at first there is only a little flickering which gradually grows, and grows, in the wrists, the elbows, now the shoulders, even the head and then OUT it comes! and flinging go the flames, flinging into the air, travelling far across the ground, now in one direction, now in another, fling, twist and leap, arrive! fling, twist and leap, arrive! again – fling, twist and leap, arrive! Now on the spot, flickering again – flickering from the floor to the ceiling – out to one side; from floor to ceiling and out to one side – but now more into the floor, more into the floor (speaking more slowly) as the heavy smoke, the thick smoke swells up, curves, surrounds, engulfs; there is less of it, much less, then only a trail of smoke left – it ebbs away, away and out.

The aim here is to bring out the character of the fire devils and to help the children to increase skill and variety in their movement expression. It will be seen that this expressive work cannot be limited to section B. We make use of aspects of A, B and C all the time, but as teachers we can focus attention mainly on one aspect or section. The paragraph above could well be broken down into shorter phrases and shorter still for work in greater detail to give time for the children to explore different ways of moving, for instance, what kind of jumps to do, which levels to use and so on. For example, 'flinging into the air' – flinging elbows? wrists? hair? – how, where in the air? high? very near, the ground? how else? flinging sideways? turning and flinging? fling, and fling and FLING, turn gather (several times) or 'and fling and fling and fling JUMP and land', etc., the children making up their own ways of doing the phrase or making up their own phrases.

*Use of the space* or where we move, also reveals character and mood: are the gestures large, or small, even restricted? Are they twisted, curving, or straight; does the movement go down into the floor, or lift and use the higher areas? Are the leg, head and arm extensions going out in a leaning or flying way, fluid almost uncontrolled in their effect or are they very stable directly up-down for instance? What are the typical positions of the character (arising from his habitual movement). Generally broad and wall-like, linear, arrow or pin like, or generally curved. Also, do the most important gestures he makes take place far from his body centre (as with a fussy yet ostentatious courtier in *The Great Stone Fire Eater*), or near his body centre (as would indicate fear of the reaction of the fire devils). The guiding principles in the use of floor space are (a) that the floor pattern should arise naturally from the motivation, and the movement content (b) that all the available floor area should be used in varied ways, (c) that certain areas should be the starting places or 'homes' of specific characters or groups. If there is stage space available, this could be used for the fire devils' mountain or South wind's domain, China, or, with the floor in front, the place for the statue.

D. *Partner and/or group work* is more obvious and perhaps more obviously essential in drama teaching though sometimes the richness of opportunity in group work is missed. Here there are to consider movement happenings of leading and following; adapting to the group, focus within and outside the group, group rhythm, development of mimetic or occupational action, as in the working scene of *The Great Stone Fire Eater*, group tensions and how members of the groups can affect each other. Also the possibilities of different group formations can be explored, and the way a group can form, such as in wedge, square, fan, or half-moon shape as circle, a line or in irregular patterns. In oriental themes, frieze-like groups and awareness of silhouette and spaces between people can be developed. Finally:

E. *Form* which, briefly, includes movement flow and rhythm, phrasing, composition ideas or how we structure our movement motifs.

## Style of movement

There are, of course, specific techniques for the different forms of Eastern dance, and it is not suggested that the children should have to imitate any of these. However, they may be interested in attempting some of the movement ideas especially for instance, in the dances, acrobatics or ritual sequences to welcome the Emperor or dragon. In ritual sequences, angles at wrist, knees and ankles have to be aimed at, with as flat a side to side movement as possible. The older children enjoying experimenting with dances such as the Indonesian candle dance, saucers balanced on hands (cymbals on each hand with thongs through to hold to avoid crashes all over the room are useful here). If anyone can be found to do this, a visit to the school of someone from an Eastern country who can perform some of the dances, or even attempt a few of the gestures for the children, would be of value. For further information on oriental dancing see book list.

## Speech work

This can be included in several ways. There can be a narrator, or group of narrators; the Emperor and his advisers can discuss matters. Vocal sound and/or words can be introduced to accompany the fire when it is in action and hissing out when it is dying in the water and to accompany the dragon, with or without additional percussion instruments.

Here is an example of some of the speeches a narrator, or group if preferred, might need to make, a group of children or the whole class of course contributing to the final version unless for some reason one child has made a version the class wishes to use.

FIRST NARRATOR (*at the beginning*): The Great Stone Fire Eater or how the fire devils were expelled from the city of San Huai.

SECOND NARRATOR: The city of San Huai was ruled by an Emperor. His court was known far and wide for the splendour of its seven gates.

*Gong.*

FIRST NARRATOR: The gate of the Lotus blossom

SECOND NARRATOR: The Iron gate

FIRST NARRATOR: The Hanging gate

SECOND NARRATOR: The gate of Jade

FIRST NARRATOR: The gate of the Golden link

SECOND NARRATOR: And there was nothing the people of the Emperor's court enjoyed more than passing through these gates. (*Music has faded in and some court people enter.*)

And again, before the entrance of the Emperor and other courtiers:

NARRATOR: Today is the Emperor's birthday and the people came to honour him.

and before the first entry of the fire devils:

NARRATOR: But the people live in fear of the terrible fire devils from the North.

and after their exit:

FIRST NARRATOR: The fire caused so much havoc that it was decided to send for the fire eating dragon(s) of China.

SECOND NARRATOR: And the people of the court prepared for their arrival with dances.

An alternative beginning, using narrator, might be:

NARRATOR: This is the story of the Great Stone Fire Eater.

*Gong.*

Our scene is set, long ago in an Eastern Kingdom, constantly threatened by death and destruction.

*Gong.*

NARRATOR: The Emperor (*He enters.*)

The people (*They enter.*)
The fire devils (*They enter and people react away.*)
The dragon (*He enters and people react towards.*)
The Great Stone Fire Eater (*Dramatic action begins.*)

## Music and sound effects

As suggested previously, use can be made of vocal sound and percussion. Korean, Chinese, Japanese and other oriental music such as Balinese should be listened to and appropriate percussion and home-made instruments selected. The teacher can encourage the use of specifically Chinese/Japanese phrasing and such devices referred to earlier as getting faster note repetitions. Extracts from oriental music might be used, as for instance a piece of Japanese Koto music for the dances. With some classes the teacher might find he needs to provide at least some of the accompaniment, but with others, groups of children will be able to invent entirely their own. The movements of the fire, the dragon and the working actions are perhaps there most obviously suited to percussion accompaniment in addition to limited use of gong and drum for the Emperor.

## Art and Craft

Here there is opportunity for making masks and headdresses, also other ornamental ingredients such as flower elbow tassels for a group of court ladies. These are simply paper flowers sewn on to tapes at least eighteen inches long, and fastened round the elbows. Some children enjoy moving with them and interesting clear gestures result. Also large fans can be made and ornamental banners (i.e. fans at least the size of a large LP record cover. It is fun making up dances with two of these, one in each hand). Some of the fire devils could have lengths of cloth which they shake, crash, flick to represent and sound like fire (but the material has to be of the right quality and size to make this effect work. The teacher needs to experiment himself before presenting the idea to the class). If the idea is adopted, dyeing of the cloth to achieve fire effects could be attempted. Shadow or rod puppets could be made and used to entertain the Emperor or dragon.

This story could give rise to the introduction of style and exploration of subject matter concerning the background life and folklore of one or more Eastern countries, each distinct; such as Korea, China, Japan, Cambodia, Bali, India, Pakistan, Burma, Ceylon, Indonesia, Thailand, or the 7,000 islands of the Philippines. Study areas could be chosen from music, art, architecture, writing, costume, dance, folklore (customs/legends), literature (and of course drama), life then and now, explorers' contact with the country (see below for further details), religion and beliefs of the people (then and now), influence of the country on England (e.g. introduction of products such as tea) and for the teacher and older primary or secondary children, influence on contemporary arts (e.g. Balanchine's ballet *Bunraku*, Tetley's ballet *Embrace Tiger and Return to Mountain*, or Boulez' instrumentation of *Le Marteau sans maître* or any of Britten's oriental-inspired works).

The characteristic movement and speech expression of the Eastern people will then infiltrate the drama work and stimulate ideas.

How can the beginner teacher set about equipping himself and the children for this task? The following suggestions have proved helpful: Read a modern account of the civilization/society. Consult standard histories of dance/dance-drama/drama. Consult encyclopaedias. Consult current Pelican book lists. Study visual arts of the area. Discover sources of folk music. Consult relevant embassy. Consult local librarian. Consult museums as/if available. Consult Geographical magazines. (For further details see book list at the end of the section.)

The teacher will find much of this information of direct use in the classroom, some will need to be abbreviated or put in simpler form for the children. It is important to provide adequate suitable visual and reading material for the children before a topic such as this is launched. Then the children can really be encouraged to follow their interests and discover things about the life of the people as background for their drama.

## BOOK LIST

To provide background study for the drama or dance drama on Korean Legend, The Great Stone Fire Eater, and to extend interest, including some books relating to China and Japan.

Faubion Bowers, *Theatre in the East*, Peter Owen

Ted Shawn, *Gods Who Dance*, Dutton
William Ridgeway, *Dramas and Dramatic Dances of non-European races*, Blom
Ashihara, *The Japanese Dance*, Japan Publications
Alan C. Heyman, *Dance of the thousand league land* (A Dance Perspective paperback) See bibliography of this book for further specialist study
R. Garfias, *The Music and Dances of the Japanese Imperial Household*, N.Y.
A. C. Scott, *Classical Theatre of China; The Kabuki Theatre of Japan*, George Allen and Unwin
*The Classical Theatre of the People: Republic of China*, published by Britain–China Friendship Association, 228 Gray's Inn Road, W.C.1
S. Obratsov, *The Chinese Puppet Theatre*, Faber and Faber

Also see relevant material in:
Curt Sachs, *World History of the Dance*, W. Norton & Co.
Mary Clarke, *Presenting People who Dance*, Paul Hamlyn
Meerloo, *Dance craze and sacred dance*, Peter Owen
Grove, *Dictionary of Music and Musicians*, Macmillan
Geographical magazines
Homer Hulbert, *History of Korea*, Routledge and Kegan Paul
L. H. Underwood, *Fifteen years among the topknots*, Boston
C. Osgood, *The Koreans and their culture*
A. D. Peterson, *The Far East – a social geography*, Duckworth
Ivan Morris, *The World of the Shining Prince*, Oxford University Press
*Larousse encyclopaedia of mythology*, Paul Hamlyn
Legends of China, Japan, Korea, etc.
Arthur Waley, Ezra Pound, and others for translations of Chinese poetry and Noh Plays
Helen Gardner, *Art Through the Ages*, G. Bell and Sons
Speltz, *Styles of Ornament*, Dover Publications Inc.
Peter Swann, *Art of China, Korea and Japan*, Thames and Hudson
R. T. Paine and A. Soper, *Art and architecture of Japan*, Penguin Books
L. Sickman and A. Soper, *Art and architecture of China*, Penguin Books
Unesco publication, *Man through his art: Music*, pages 24, 34, 44, E. P. Publishing Co.
See *Encyclopaedia Britannica* for many aspects of life – e.g. Chinese writing.

## EXPLORERS

Since the legend from Korea and Eastern life and cultures in general have been the focus of interest for the last section, here are some suggestions which the teacher can follow concerning some explorers who have visited the area. From studying children's characteristics we know that curiosity and interest in exploration are prevalent. Therefore, from the age of about nine years upwards, stories concerning explorers are excellent teacher-initiated subject matter for drama –

drama develops well from the lives of these people and has the value of factual, true-story human content which provides a good balance to legendary or fantasy themes. As stated previously, these teacher-initiated themes take place concurrently with the children's own drama and improvisation with and without music.

The theme of exploration has much in common with children as they discover their own world. The earliest travellers and explorers were simply men spreading out across the earth in order to live. But men have always been inquisitive. Sometimes the journeys were tentative or surreptitious, sometimes bold, sometimes driven on by hostile tribes. In early times men relied on the stars to guide them and simple canoes or boats. Arrival was even sometimes by accident. Later, travellers went specifically in search of trade, or for religious conversion, acquisition of land, or scientific discovery, or knowledge about other parts of the world – curiosity.

Some explorers who visited the East:

*Chang Ch'ien*: one of the earliest known Chinese travellers. In the Second Century B.C. he was sent out by the Emperor Wu Ti of the Han dynasty and his reports resulted in the opening of the Silk Route from the Gobi to Khotan, to Harkand and Ferghana. He was imprisoned by the Huns on two occasions, once for ten years, once for twelve years.

*Hsüan Tsang*: of China (?A.D. 605–664) who was a scholarly Buddhist wanting to travel in order to fill gaps in his knowledge of the sacred books. Although forbidden permission to leave China he was encouraged by a dream and set out and in A.D. 629 crossed the Gobi desert. He reached the camp of the Great Khan having crossed the ice bound Tien Shan. Eventually he reached Kashmir and travelled over India. He had collected manuscripts and flower seeds on his travels but lost them on his way across the Punjab. Sixteen years after he had left his country he was welcomed back in spite of his illegal departure and he handed all his manuscripts and treasures to his Monastery.

*John de Carpini* (1182–1252) of Italy sent by the Pope to the Great Khan. He travelled the 3,000 miles on horseback.

*William Rubruquis* (William of Rubruck, 1215–70) of France who travelled across Central Asia mainly by cart. (For the above two explorers see *The Journey of William of Rubruck to the Eastern Parts of the World 1253–55* as narrated by himself, and two accounts of the *Early Journey of John Pain de Carpini* translated by W. Woodville Rockhill, Hakluyt Society, London.)

*Niccolo and Maffeo Polo* jewel merchants. Visited the Great Khan, and travelled near present day Peking.

*Marco Polo* (1254–1324) of Venice (Son of Niccolo) (see following section).

*Ibn Batuta* of Morocco (1304–77?) Amongst other places, 1325–49 visited N.W. India, Delhi, Bengal, and the Ganges delta, Ceylon, Sumatra and Peking. A considerable traveller, by the time he died he had travelled about 75,000 miles. (See *Ibn Batuta: Travels in Asia and Africa 1325–54*, translated by H. A. R. Gibb, Routledge.)

*Ferdinand Magellan* of Portugal (1480?–1521) 1501–12 visited the Malay archipelago and Sumatra. On a later voyage he visited the Philippines, where he was killed. The story of Magellan, that of a tragic hero, is an especially potent one with excellent opportunities for drama. One important element in the tragedy is the jealous rivalry of Portugal and Spain, both pioneers in the new seaways opening up, and greedily seeking wealth. (See Zweig, *Magellan.*)

*Diego Lopez de Sequira* of Portugal – 1509 having sailed to Calicut with Magellan and Seirano, he crossed the Bay of Bengal to the Malacca coast and sailed around Sumatra.

*Francisco Seirano* of Portugal (who it is thought influenced Magellan to find his way round the World), 1511 went to North Java and the islands beyond. Stayed there for the rest of his life in the service of the Prince of Terna.

*Francis Xavier* of Spain (1506–52) a Jesuit priest. 1540–52 set out from Europe and rounded the Cape to India. In 1549 he went to Japan, the first recorded Christian missionary to do so. Went through the Strait of Malacca to the spice islands and Ternate. He eventually landed in China, and sailed on to Japan.

*Sir Francis Drake* of England (1541?–90) In 1579 he sailed to the Philippines, the spice islands across the Indian Ocean and around the Cape of Good Hope.

*William Dampier* of England (1652–1715), 1679 visited the Philippines and Cochin China, amongst other places.

Selected book references are included above, and as these indicate, when preparing work of this kind, consult and use the first hand reports, diaries, etc., of the explorers or travellers, or their companions.

## MARCO POLO

The story of Marco Polo is one of the great sagas of our history and like most of the topics in this chapter, should not be attempted if time is limited. The method suggested here is to begin with various studies by groups of children on the background of the times. Their findings will be shared with the class and used in the playmaking. If suitable books are available, the children can read the story of the journey for themselves. To prepare for the scenes the teacher will need to study books listed at the end of this section. Some references to these books are included in the following suggestions.

### Suggestions for scenes

*Introduction*: Marco waiting on the quayside, Venice, hoping his father and uncle will return.

1. A lively scene can be developed using the character of Martino de Canale who wrote a book *In Praise of Venice* at the time. He describes the procession of the Guilds. Marco can be with a friend, talking to Martino, awaiting the procession. He will mention his father and uncle and the land of the Tartars. All he knows is that his father went to the land of the Tartars.[6]
2. '*The Tartars are Coming*' The authentic story of Friar John Carpini who went to the Tartar headquarters Kara Korum with a message of peace from the Pope in 1341, can be used. He describes his meeting with a group of Tartars in the night, when he had reached South Russia. Their horsemanship, and power as warriors can be shown.[6]

*The Journey*

1. The three Polos at Acre: the friars turn back. Marco's father, at the request of Kublai Khan, whom he had come to respect greatly while in Cathay, had promised to bring back 100 Christian teachers. The Great Khan felt that the ideas of Christians would help his people as

he now regarded the people of Cathay. He was a grandson of the terrible Jenghis Khan, but totally different, a wise, highly intelligent man of sensitive perceptions yet being a Tartar, a great war leader.

To the great disappointment of the travellers, (Niccolo, father, Matteo, uncle, and Marco) the two friars they had managed to bring away with them turned back. This happened at Acre.[7]

2. Escape from a sandstorm. As they near the Persian Gulf, expecting to take ship from there, a blinding sand storm envelops them. A lively scene can be developed, with shouts of the raiders, cries of the people making the journey. The three men escape.[8]
3. On the 'Roof of the World'. This scene on the mighty Tiber Plateau can be used to relate previous adventures since they turned back from the Persian Gulf, deciding the ships there were not sea-worthy: or use in narration.[9]

*In Cathay*

1. First meeting in Peking. Festival with Kublai Khan presiding. There is ample information to make this scene when Marco is introduced to the Great Khan, an exciting one. A Festival is in progress with dancers, conjurers, etc. The Khan is impressed by the young man, grieved that the 100 Christians have not arrived.[10]
2. Marco reports to Kublai Khan. Marco became a trusted friend of the Khan, made many journeys on his behalf, bringing back reports.

   This scene can reveal some aspects of life in South China. He found an old-established Christian group there. Religious toleration was practised in ancient China and under Kublai Khan. He also found a 'Venice' more wonderful than his own.[11]

*Return*

1. Marco in prison in Jenod. In the war between Venice and Genoa, Marco was, after his return, made prisoner. He dictated his famous story while in prison. But for this the world would not have known of the news he brought back of a totally unknown civilization.
2. Marco clowned at a Venice festival. His stories seemed so fantastic they nicknamed him 'Il Milione' suggesting he wildly exaggerated in talking of thousands of temples, etc. So it became a regular feature at local festivals to do a 'clowning' act of Marco Polo. In fact he spoke the truth with remarkable clarity, exactly as he saw it.

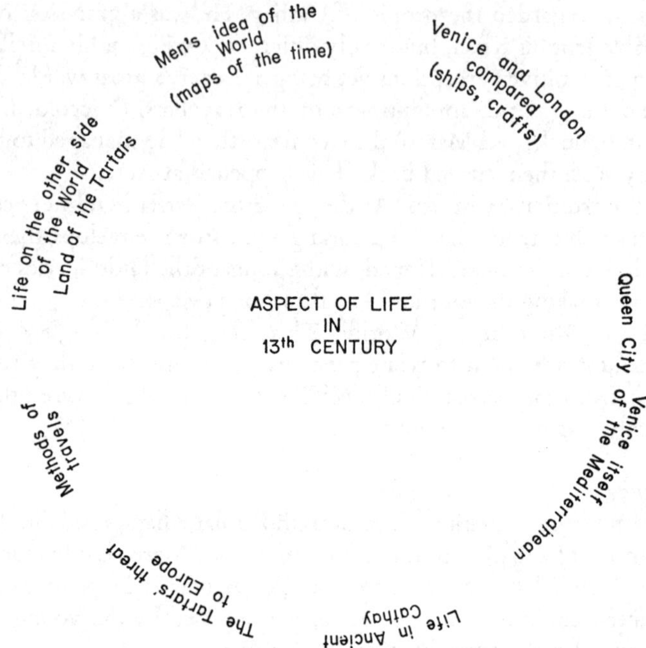


**Suggestions for Work to do as background for drama**

1. Follow Marco Polo's journey on a globe, and on wall and atlas maps, and make your own map to show his route.
2. Find out what animals are used for desert transport. Draw them and explain why man chooses them.
3. Describe and draw the wild sheep of the Pamirs.
4. Find out all you can about Persia (Iran) as it is today, and as it was in Marco Polo's time.
5. Pretending you are Marco Polo, write a diary of your travels.
6. Or write a story about a part of your travels – pretending you are Marco Polo.
7. Write about the desert cities Marco visited.
8. Make a sketch map to show where the Gobi Desert is, and write in your own words all you can find out about it.
9. Before going to sleep at night the men of the caravan would find their direction and set a mark. How?

10. From what did the Chinese make paper money? Why did Marco Polo think it so useful?
11. Copy out what Marco Polo says about some black stones he found. Is his description quite correct?
12. Write out what Marco Polo said about the Yangtse. Find out all you can about it.
13. Find out all you can about: junks, pagodas, rice, silk, sago, bamboo, coconuts, spices, Chinese food, pepper, cinnamon, Chinese clothing, camphor, monsoons, ginger, nutmegs.
14. Find out about the Great Wall of China, then write about it in your book.

BOOK LIST

Eileen Power, *Medieval People,* Pelican Books 1937
M. B. Synge, *A Book of Discovery*, Thomas Nelson & Sons
*Great Plain of China*, Longmans Colour Geographies, Unit 9, 1957 (suitable for children 10–13)
*The Travels of Marco Polo*, translated by R. E. Latham, Penguin Books, 1958
Maurice Collis, *Marco Polo*, Faber and Faber, 1950
Marion Koenig, *The Travels of Marco Polo*, Paul Hamlyn, 1964 (written and illustrated for children)
*Marco Polo*, Ladybird Book.
Other books are given in Introduction to the Penguin translation.

## COLUMBUS

A child may recall the Columbus story by the ditty,

In fourteen hundred and ninety-two,
Columbus sailed the ocean blue.

However, is it not in fact totally unsuited to be linked with such a jingle? It is in the first place, the tragic drama of a man 'possessed' by a dream to the end of his life. It also reveals how the pursuit of this dream led to the tragedy of a vast continent: suddenly assailed by powerful strangers, the slowly-evolving ways of life of its peoples, ended for ever. It is of course, also a turning point in world history.

Put like this, the theme may seem unsuitable for children of this age range. This may be so, but on the other hand, are there many stories of any depth not open to this comment?

If a theme like 'Columbus' is chosen, the teacher should not falsify its realities to suit the age of the children, but rather, make wise selection of the material, and 'open the door' to the child's own reflections. This opportunity has been taken to mention a point of view applicable to many stories the children hear, not least among them some of the New Testament, whose deeper meanings go far beyond their immediate grasp.

Unless otherwise stated, references are to *Christopher Columbus* by Salvador Madariaga. For the children's reading there is *Columbus Sails* (a Puffin paperback), by Walter Hodges.

To assist the teacher in preparing background for dramatic work, here are some notes on salient facts in the story:

*Boyhood.* Born 1451 in port of Genoa (of Marco Polo fame). His father was a wool weaver. Two of his brothers were intimately connected with his life, especially a younger one, Bartholomew. Christopher is described as a lad with red hair, sunburnt freckled skin and blue eyes. His biographer accepts the evidence that he was of Jewish descent, but he felt himself to be a devout member of the Christian Church. He was apprenticed to the weaving craft though irresistibly drawn to ships and the sea. Both he and Bartholomew began their association with the sea as boys, Christopher at ten. 'The ship was his School, Lisbon his University'. He began navigating at fourteen, picking up his astronometrical notations at the ropes. Almanacks and books on astrology may have lain about in the Captain's berth. At nineteen he was helping his father to pay off debts. For the next six years he seems to have been mainly at sea. Then came 1476 and a crisis in his life. The French corsair (pirate) ship he had joined was set fire in a battle with Genoese, and wrecked. Being a great swimmer, he was able to reach land. He landed at the very foot of the Rock of Sagres, jutting out from the Portuguese coast into the unknown ocean, the rock where Prince Henry the Navigator had built his famous centre. For the next eight years his life was centred on Lisbon, a city 'throbbing with the fever of discovery'. Madariaga vividly describes the atmosphere – the busy Street of the Merchants, the shops with wine, fish, cinnamon, tar . . . the talk in the streets, on the quayside about sea journeys along the African coast, about the way to the Spice Islands. . . . and. . . . the bookshops. Lisbon was a city of learning. In these shops were charts, books, books about astronomy and cosmography, astrolabes, compasses and sandclocks. In such a shop Christopher found his young brother Bartholomew, still in his teens, busily engaged in the work of making painted maps for the use of sailors, 'correctly drawn', showing seas, coasts, bays, islands 'in their true proportions'. Their two lives were interlinked from now onwards.

## Events leading up to the Voyage

1. *1476 to 1784 in Portugal.* The following developments may be noted:

(a) Columbus went to sea for various reasons during this period. In 1477 he went as far as Iceland, 'the last of the lands'. Probably his life purpose to cross the unknown ocean to reach the Great Khan's land had already set fire to his imagination. Marco Polo's book dominated his thoughts.

(b) He evidently studied every relevant book and map he could lay his hands on making notes in margins. He sought out men known to have been on adventurous voyages. He studied the ways of calculating the distances between lines of longitude. So this 'Dreamer', this 'Don Quixote', as some have called him (with reason), was searching for certain facts with dedicated zeal.

(c) He married into a family of wealth and high position; and it gave him an invaluable advantage, as members of the family had rights in the island of Porto Santo, an admirable base for exploring the Western Sea. It seems he went to live there.

(d) He gathered evidence of the existence of land far west of the ocean.

(e) A strange attitude to the planned voyage formed in his mind. He decided that in asking for help from the King, he would make certain demands; that when he reached his goal, he should have one tenth of all the income 'accruing to the King' from the fabulous wealth in gold, pearls, spices, etc., that would be acquired. In addition he should be known as the Admiral of Castille, should be 'perpetual Viceroy and Governor' of all the discovered lands . . . and be entitled to wear golden spurs. (The biographer gives an explanation of these claims, relating them to the treatment the Jewish people were receiving at this time.) There is no doubt that he firmly believed he was called by God to cross the ocean.

(f) The Court made fun of him. The King refused to give help. With his small son, Diego, he left for Spain. His wife had died.

Before leaving he had secretly entered a Library, and copied the Toscanelli map.

## Suggestions for planning dramatic work

1. *In the Bookshop, Lisbon* – content can include:

(a) Contrasts between the brothers. Christopher self-engrossed, impulsive, positive, sometimes passionate. The younger brother, Bartholomew, quiet, reliable.
(b) The intense interest of C in all kinds of books and maps, navigation instruments. Conversation between them can show that new maps are the talk of the town. One or more sailors and ships' captains may enter, with Africa and the chance of wealth from the spice trade *their* preoccupation.
(c) C's approaching marriage, and the opportunities it will bring.
(d) C's experience at sea: escape from drowning at Sagres, recent visit to Iceland and what he felt when he looked west from its coast. A crowded shop listens, sceptical.
(e) A hint of the claims that C. will make, when he asks for aid from the King.

2. *The Court derides*

A quite different scene. Ladies and gentlemen talk, laugh, dance; Columbus enters; noticeable reactions. Perhaps his wife is with him, and dances with one of the fine gentlemen. Meanwhile Columbus, not aware that they think his ideas foolish, and his claims outrageous, is drawn into talk about his intentions. They laugh at his floating 'evidence' of land westwards: he tells of the strange corpses and carved wood. At least one lady refuses to believe the world is round.

3. *Columbus secretly copies the map*

And now further notes on the next part of the story and suggestions for dramatic work: 1484 to 1492. In Spain.

For the next eight years Columbus sought the help of the King and Queen of Spain, the famous Ferdinand and Isabella. There is certainly opportunity for dramatic activity. These two rulers were distinctive and interesting personalities. They set up a Commission of wise men who considered and dismissed his appeal. The King was preoccupied with the final defeat of the Moslems, who had long dominated Spain. A scene with the Queen talking with Columbus, in the presence of people of the

Court, is a possibility; or one showing him being interviewed by the Commission. In the latter, the case against his plan could be presented. His plea was rejected (after four long years). He appealed again to the Queen with no success. He had however made some powerful friends, among them Martin Pinzon, a wealthy man, an experienced sea captain, and moreover, one smitten with the fever of sea discovery.

In January 1492, having found a haven in a friendly monastery, he decided to leave Spain, intending to make an appeal elsewhere. He rode away, looking (but doubtless not feeling) like a beggar, in poor threadbare clothes. He reached the Bridge of Pinos, eight miles out of Granada. Meanwhile powerful friends had been to the Queen. As he was crossing the bridge a swift horseman overtook him, with a message from the Queen. As his biographer says, 'he returned to Santa Fe – and immortality', certain that the Lord had sent the messenger.

We can imagine Columbus resting on the bridge, when the sound of a galloping horse is heard. The rider recognizes him, dismounts, and comes running towards him. Meanwhile passers-by have no doubt lingered on the bridge, noticed the rather odd stranger, and commented. They are likely to be curious about the Queen's messenger speaking to this man. They probably find various explanations, all wide of the mark. So Columbus has won at last. Three ships are given him, and his extravagant claims are accepted. On 3rd August the three little ships, *Santa Maria, Pinta* and *Nina* set sail. Martin Pinzon is with him.

One or two scenes of the voyage can be planned. The Puffin paperback, *Columbus Sails*, uses a sailor's story to describe the voyage and the arrival. The children can get many ideas from it. (Brian Way's play *Columbus Sails*, *Columbus* by Louis MacNeice, *The Age of Discovery* by Rhoda Power, and 'four voyages of Columbus' (Penguin) for teachers.)

## Suggestions for scenes

(a) *September 9th. The Canaries are left behind.*
It is recorded that two boys and certain old sailors wept when the last known land was left behind.

(b) *Mutiny threatens*
The sailors at night talk together, plan action. They speak of Pinzon, guessing he would use ruthless action to quell revolt.

(c) *October 11th*
Columbus had sworn on the crucifix that if by the third midnight no land is sighted, they will turn back. At 10 o'clock on the 11th Columbus sees a light ahead. He talks excitedly with two sailors about it. Sailors talk together through the night, about the birds seen and the crab! Their fears are still in their hearts.

(d) *Early Morning, October 12th*
This famous scene which surely will still be told through the centuries ahead to school children, can hardly be omitted. The Pinta gunshot rings out. One man has seen land! No doubt the reader remembers the story of that fateful early morning, when a vast continent totally unknown before, ended its seclusion from the rest of the world.

(e) *The Landing*
The triumphal landing is made. The 'Admiral' is in armour with a crimson cloak. The captains of the two other ships, Martin and Vincent Pinzon carry green and white flags. Columbus carries the Royal Standard of Spain. He springs into the surf, strides over the white sand, kneels and prays. Rising he calls on all to witness, as he strikes the ground with the Royal Banner that this new land is claimed for Their Majesties Ferdinand and Isabella. The sailors can now see that the beach is marked with footprints. Men of the island who had crowded on to the beach when the ships first approached, have disappeared.

The meeting, and exchange of the Spanish bells, beads, etc., for parrots, gold ornament and cotton balls has fascination and pathos; knowing as we do now of the disasters that followed it.

Columbus feels sure, mistakenly, that he has reached the islands of Cipango, and the lands of the Great Khan lie ahead. (Later on when they reach Cuba, the word for Mid-Cuba, 'Cubana*can*' convinces him that they are in the domains of this great ruler.) Nothing can change his certainty that the land of Marco Polo is reached.

## Briefly, the end of the story

Columbus claims many islands for Ferdinand and Isabella.

The *Pinta* sails off in search of gold; Columbus too. (Columbus always treats the chief with great ceremony.)

Powerful Chief Guacanagari sends presents and messengers who invite Columbus to see him. The man at the helm falls asleep, therefore the ship goes on to a sandbank. Guancanagari's people help to right the vessel. Guacanagari gives permission for a Spanish fortress in Hispaniola. A banquet. Columbus leaves 39 men at the fortress.

*Pinta* and *Nina* after cruising round the islands, leave for Spain.

Bad weather. *Nina* shelters in Portugal. (*Pinta* reached Spain first.) The Portuguese think Columbus has discovered India, and are angry and jealous. However, they pretend friendship. Triumphant return of Columbus. Many young men wish to join him on another voyage. Columbus assures them that the kingdom of the Great Khan is near 'his' islands.

The next voyage: 17 vessels and 1,500 men but they find the fortress left on Hispaniola in ruins. The crew are undisciplined and greedy. They treat the gentle Indians unkindly and rebel against Columbus. Some steal ships and return to Spain to spread evil reports. Columbus is not given such a pleasant reception on his return this time.

The Spanish king grows jealous of the Portuguese who had found India by this time. Columbus is therefore sent West again. He sails down the coasts of N. and S. America still thinking he is approaching the lands of the Khan. Full of grief at the bad treatment of the Indians, he contracts fever. He is marooned for a year in Jamaica. Promises made to him were not kept: his 'followers' took what should have been his.

1506 – Columbus died at Valladrid, an embittered man. He never knew he had found a new continent.

## INDIANS

### Peoples of the Unknown Continent

The purpose of this part is to give some idea of the very varied communities which had been living and developing for unknown centuries in the American Continent isolated from the rest of the world. The discovery by Columbus was to lead to the destruction of their ways of life, an unbelievably tragic human experience to follow so gallant an endeavour.

### Suggested Method

The so-called Indians, living in widely different environments, had naturally developed distinctive ways of living. The plan proposed is to consider five groups, the Sioux, the Seneca, the Makah and the Zuni, all of North America, and the Incas of Peru in South America.

It is suggested that each group in the class shall take one of these, and find ways to describe their way of life. After class discussion dramatic activity can follow each presentation, involving if suitable, other members of the class.

A book by an American, Benjamin Brester, *The First Book of Indians* and Christopher Davis, *North American Indian* are two books of many, useful to both teacher and children.

There is ample opportunity for varied activities in such a theme – maps, drawings, models, preparations of clothes, implements, etc., of use in the scenes.

A relief map showing the natural vegetation, forests, grasslands, deserts is a necessity. Each group will need copies and may make their own special maps for the area chosen.

Notes on each group of Indians. The intention here is merely to emphasize leading points which the teacher may need in order to give direction.

## The Sioux (pronounced 'Soo')

(This is the only one of the five groups whose life is described in the book referred to above after the coming of Europeans, when horses had been introduced into the continent. For the purpose of this theme, the buffalo hunts are described here as they were originally.)

*Background: The famous Prairies (grasslands) of central North America*

(a) The buffalo (bison) fed on the grass, moved north in the summer and southwards as winter approached, in vast herds. Indian tribes in this region had become dependent on these animals for their needs. Hence they followed the herds.

(b) Thus the Sioux were nomadic, moving with all their belongings, but settling in one place for the winter.

(c) The hunt was central to their lives. Their weapons were bows and arrows; they often used a particular stone arrowhead. The method used was as follows:

(i) a special ceremony was held, after which scouts went off to find the herd. A method of signalling enabled them to tell the camp when it was located.

(ii) the usual method then was for one group of hunters to isolate some of the animals, forcing them to run in one direction, while the other hunters approached them as they ran. Confusion followed and many animals were killed.
(iii) the many uses of the buffalo are fully described in the book mentioned above.
(iv) other points of interest are: clothes, tents, women's work, strenuous training of hunters, preparation of meat, absence of cultivated crops, use of dogs.

Opportunities for dramatic activity include: (a) the hunt; (b) winter scene in the tepee (tent), round the fire. Mother and girls busy making baskets, etc. Grandfather (and grandmother) tell stories. Hunts and wars with other tribes may be talked about. (Also see *The Sioux*.[12])

## Seneca Indians

Background: the hilly wooded country behind present-day New York.

An excellent account in the book of reference gives ample information, showing how the very different natural conditions affected the life of the people.

Special features: permanent settlement, more varied life (hunting, farming, canoeing, fighting, playing, singing). The importance of maize (corn). The men liked hats – fancy skull caps, each with one large eagle feather, fastened on so that it whirled in the wind.

*Dramatic Opportunities*

(a) The hunt of the deer
(b) Dances – 'before battle' dance, 'The False Face Club' dance (meaning masks were worn for complete disguise)
(c) Games (i) Lacrosse (ii) 'Snow Snake': a large pole with one heavy end was sent over snow (a good throw might go as far as ¼ mile) (iii) children's games
(d) Women preparing food: (i) sugar from maple (ii) grinding corn as they sing.
(e) The 'burying of the hatchet' after a tribal fight, with use of sign language.

## Makah Indians

Background: the Pacific coastland of present-day State of Washington.

This of course is a totally different setting from the others. The great wealth was in fish, especially salmon. Hence they could trade with others for furs, etc. They were relatively wealthy.

*Special Features and Dramatic Opportunities*

Sea travel in huge canoes dug out of the great cedar trees, capture of whales with harpoon: methods of preserving fish; their large houses with 'bunks'; their beliefs, celebrations, use of slaves, fights, practice spear throwing for salmon and harpooning whales. Suggested scene: the 'potlatch' or celebration, when the 'greatest' man was he who gave away the most – though ostentatiously and with pride.

## Zuni Indians of the desert country (present-day New Mexico)

Desert People.

*Special points*

(a) Here the need for water is a large factor in the life of the community. Strange examples can be found of this: they were great runners and in travelling often ran, believing it would help the water in their rivers to flow.

(b) They lived in a 'pueblo', with houses built one on top of the other. There were no windows (a protection from enemies) so ladders were used to climb up.

(c) They irrigated the land and grew crops, corn being one of them.

(d) The women were skilled in cooking, had ovens outside and inside houses, made bread from wheat. They even had chewing gum.

(e) They used to meet in an upper room kept for the purpose. Here they held ceremonies sometimes serious, sometimes with clowning performances; these rooms were often used for weaving and conversation.

## Notes on Sign Language

The different Indian groups usually spoke their own language, so they developed 'signs' as a means of communication. Some are shown in the book of reference. It is suggested that the scene (Seneca Indians Scene (e)) when burying of the hatchet is enacted, the children can try to use these signs and perhaps invent others in scenes of their own.

## Notes on use of drums, masks, head-dresses, etc.

As in other primitive dramas, music in these scenes is an integral part of the enactment and usually consists of rhythmic pattern and chant to assist the build-up of tension, to support the action, or to operate as a counterpoint to action. The drums may speak a language of their own and children enjoy composing their own drum messages and rhythms. Certain instruments can accompany certain characters in the drama. Moreover, as mentioned previously, the tribal Indian dancers use masks to transform themselves, and children enjoy doing the same and exert considerable skill in constructing unusual profiles and facial patterns. Half masks, but extending above and round the sides of the head are usually the best for energetic work, as they are more comfortable to wear.

Teachers should experiment themselves with masks before encouraging their use with children. The mask is a powerful object, and the teacher needs to know the kind of sensation it can induce in the wearer before suggesting their indiscriminate use. It is interesting to find out about the use of masks in other primitive cultures. In some African tribes the masks are fetish objects and women cannot look at them without risking death. Children enjoy making their own headdresses and equivalents of decorated ceremonial objects such as shields, emblems to use in their dramas. Also the idea of important aspects of their lives being painted on the walls of caves can be utilized, either as background to the drama, or if a home or tribal base is needed, to indicate this on a screen behind or around the action – (just as children in the Infants' department decorate their home corner). Incidentally, as many teachers know, it is possible for children to construct homes on the lines of those used by primitive peoples of the country they are studying.

## **The Incas** (members of the Quechua society)

Quite another world is reached in studying the Incas, and the teacher is bound to spend time in preparation. An excellent book to use is *The Inca Indians of the Andes*[13]. For more detailed information there is *The Last of the Incas*[14].

Space does not permit more than a few brief points:

(a) Here was one of the most extraordinary civilizations of history. It can be described as a highly organized welfare state run on totalitarian lines (to use our modern terms).

Organization was the binding thread that held it together, with the discipline that went with it from childhood to maturity. The Emperor, son of the Sun God, was the all-powerful ruler.

(b) Special features of this civilization: (i) the Great Highways (ii) the markets (iii) the use of 'terraces' and irrigation on steep mountain slopes (iv) the great ceremonies, each month, especially in June – the Festival of the Sun (v) the poetic quality of prayers to the Creator, and to other gods such as the Earth Mother (vi) the importance of the llama in transport (vii) training for war (viii) the 'runners' – compulsory service for this for limited period (ix) the strong element of co-operation.

*Suggested scenes*

1. *Going to Market*

Men, women and children are going along the highway. They are passed by runners. Talk is of the market they will soon reach. Night comes, they settle down on mats to sleep. Special incidents can be used, for example, the little daughter's concern for her ducks, the boy's interest in trading and the use of the knotted strings for keeping records. (Quipus)

2. *The Marriage Ceremony*

3. *The Festival of the Sun* (It actually took nine days)

Additional suggestion: Delaware Indians. *Dickon among the Indians*[15] relates the adventures of an English boy captured by the Delaware Indians. He is trained in tribal ways. This book could be used as a basis for work similar to the above.

## INTRODUCING MARY KINGSLEY

This can be an exciting drama – centred theme, with as much activity of other kinds as the teacher wishes. Probably an introduction only can be achieved with children of this age.

### Notes on the background[16]

1. Mary Kingsley (1862–1900) was one of the most astonishing women of the second half of the nineteenth century, or any century. She died at 38, having not only travelled alone in Equatorial Africa, learning the ways of the people as surely no one else has done, but championing the

cause of African and British traders here in Britain with lasting effects (unknown however to her). She offered her services in the Boer War, was sent to nurse Boer prisoners in appalling conditions, caught enteric fever and died there. She was buried at sea in accordance with her own wish.
2. Her family: she was niece of Charles Kingsley; her father was a doctor with a 'Wanderlust', a courageous man whom Mary intensely admired. In her younger years he was rarely at home. Her mother had increasingly delicate health and Mary's young womanhood was almost entirely absorbed by domestic cares. She had no formal education (unlike her brothers, two years younger) but read extraordinary books such as *Murders of most notorious pirates*, books on science, and found the journal, *The English Mechanic*, quite indispensable.
3. A few details of her life. She was brought up in Highgate, and the children can create a scene from the records of the time. Later the family moved to Bexley Heath and then to Cambridge, when her brother was a student there.

Suddenly in her early thirties she was bereaved of both parents, whom she had devotedly cared for in their last, ailing years.

With the idea of continuing her father's researches into primitive religions, and of collecting specimens of fish and insects for scientific reasons, she went to equatorial West Africa, travelling alone among cannibal tribes. She loved the vast dangerous forest lands that killed so many Englishmen, and developed an intense regard and human understanding of the people,

## Suggestions for Scenes

In order to allow the children to understand something of the life in primitive West Africa, two opening scenes are suggested. They are entirely based on a remarkable book, *Born a Savage* by Prince Motupe. The writer was born in French Guinea before any contact was made in his homeland with Europeans. He writes vividly of the life of himself and his people. The book reveals intrinsic qualities of these Africans, their courage, powerful sense of loyalty to family and homeland, their harsh 'justice' to offenders of their laws.

Scene 1: Motupe hears the story of his birth.
Scene 2: Preparation for manhood
If possible drums and dances should be used in each.

Scene 1 is so vividly described in the book that no description is needed.

For Scene 2, when the boy is awaiting his 'Test of Courage' (he has to go into the forest alone, meet and conquer a large fierce animal). The whole class can be involved in the triumphal procession when, nearly dead, he is carried to the ceremony where 'manhood' is conferred upon him.

(A third scene showing the trial and death of an offender can be used.)

Scene 4: Mary Kingsley at home in Highgate, thirteen years old.

See the story of her girlhood in Stephen Gwynn's book. It can involve a number of characters, father, mother, brother and Mrs Barrett the humble little cockney maid, burglars lurking on the path nearby and of course the young girl, who in this violent scene, cleverly hides the book on 'Solar Physics' from father, until she has finished studying it.

*Other Scenes*

The scope is considerable, and only the teacher can decide which are appropriate. Scenes in Africa and on the voyage out can well be chosen such as:

(a) Mary at night freeing the leopard and meeting her amazed African friends just after this.[17]

(b) Mary in the forest with her Fan helpers. She falls in the leopard trap. Later, one of the men takes her to see a rare sight; it proves to be a family gathering of gorillas. The man sneezes at the most awkward moment.[18]

Finally a lively scene can be worked out for Mary when she has returned, giving talks and lectures all over the country, to boys at Eton, ladies in drawing rooms, in large halls in London (one in Highbury in particular).

Perhaps the Drawing Room scene would delight the children most. Mary's adventures described in her vivid manner caused many a tea cup to crash on the floor.

BOOK LIST

Prince Motupe, *Born a Savage*, O.U.P. (out of print)
Mary Kingsley, *Travels in West Africa* (out of print)

Stephen Gwynn, *The Life of Mary Kingsley*, Penguin Books 1932
Olwen Campbell, *Mary Kingsley*, Methuen 1917

*For Children's Reading*
Helen Simpson, *A Woman among Savages*, a Puffin Story Book
Jean Gordon Hughes, *Invincible Miss*, Macmillan 1968

## INTRODUCING CHARLES STURT

*Journey 1.* Sturt led exploration from Sydney – over the Great Coastal mountains – which for years defied explorers – to track rivers from their sources across the vast interior grasslands. (Usually of course rivers are explored from their mouths – but desert and other difficulties prevented this in the case of the great Murray – Darling river.)

He took boats with his party over the mountains – fitting them together when they reached rivers on the other side. They reached the place where the rivers Murray and Darling meet – returned to Sydney over the mountains again.

*Journey 2.* A fearful expedition which attempted to cross the desert from South to North from Adelaide. There are vivid descriptions of the heat and lack of water – of death of members of the expedition. Sturt became blind because of the fierce rays of the sun. They returned to Adelaide – but if only they could have gone on a little further they would have reached water. (Sturt did recover his sight partially and worked in Perth as a writer in later life.)

For further details, see the life of Sturt and history of exploration in Australia.

## MEN OF EVEREST, 1953

This theme is chosen to show how dramatic activity can illustrate a particular experience of men. It involves a team of people, working under one man's leadership to achieve a well defined end. The team-work is varied in character, arduous, often dangerous: the climax of all this preparation is in the hands of two men only, on whose judgment, courage and powers of endurance, success depends; and as these two slowly climb the last 'knife-edge' towards the summit, each man holds the other's life in his hands. Having imagined this, the children are likely to receive a deep and lasting impression.

This theme although drama-centred, offers rich opportunities for varied activities, for groups and individuals, and subjects such as:

(a) the challenge of mountains to man
(b) nature's way of 'sculpturing' the landscape, with special reference to ice action
(c) Maps, models, drawings
(d) Human life at high altitudes, with particular reference to Tenzing's homeland in Nepal, and his people's land of origin, Tibet.

There is not space here for a full description of scenes, but briefly, these could include: Tenzing's early escapades; accident (with Hillary) on the icefall attacking the summit. *Man of Everest* (biography of Tenzing)[19] will be found useful as a basis for this work. (The Everest film can be hired from the Rank agency, cost £7.10.0.)

Teachers are recommended to look up other real life stories of endeavour as a basis for drama work. In addition to autobiographies/biographies of explorers, and discoverers, see stories of escapes and rescue, for example: *Great Moments of Rescue*[20] and *The World of Espionage.*[21]

## BEOWULF

### Situation action plot

This is an epic tale, the oldest in any non-classical European language, of dramatic strength and by an unknown author. The theme of Beowulf is the conflict of good and evil. It is, too, an expression of fear of the dark, and an examination of the nature and purpose of heroism. (Thus it fulfils the demand stated earlier of classroom drama for serious underlying thematic content.) Typical of the heroic age are those positive motives for action which appeal to the Primary School child. 'It affirms the human being in a world where everything is transient' (David Wright).

The teacher should tell the children the story, and intersperse his telling with selected passages from a good translation of the original. There are many beautiful and impressive passages to choose from; the descriptions of the fights are of course especially popular with children. (For a summary of the story see the Introduction to Beowulf by David Wright in the Penguin edition.)

## Selection of passages for dramatization

There are many sections which form a basis well suited to dramatic work; to summarize these:

1. Hrothgar's rule: success in battle. The great hall of Heorot is built.
2. The grim, half-human demon Grendel, irritated by the mirth he hears, attacks Heorot and continues to do so for twelve years.
3. News of this reaches Gothland where one of Hygelac's followers, his nephew the hero Beowulf, sets out to help with fourteen companions.
4. Having travelled across the sea, Beowulf arrives, and is challenged by the coastguard. He meets courageous Wulfgar, and is welcomed by king Hrothgar, noble Queen Wealhtheow and other Danes. But envious Unferth resents Beowulf's arrival.
5. Grendel comes to Heorot and fights with Beowulf. Before his escape, Beowulf wrenches off one arm of the monster and fastens it high on the wall of Heorot.
6. Hrothgar and the chieftains arrive from far and wide to see Grendel's arm. Feasting and gifts are bestowed on Beowulf.
7. Grendel's mother comes to avenge her son, and attacks Heorot, killing Aeshere, one of the king's best-loved counsellors.
8. Beowulf goes to fight Grendel's mother in the lake, and kills her under water.
9. Feasting and further gifts.
10. Beowulf and his companions return home to Hygelac and Queen Hygd.
11. Hygelac is killed and Beowulf escapes by swimming. He refuses the crown but supports Hygelac's son, Heardred, until the death of Heardred. Beowulf rules for fifty years.
12. The threat of the dragon-guardian of treasure in an ancient sepulchral tumulus. A runaway slave has stolen a jewelled cup and the dragon is incensed.
13. The dragon, searching for the thief, attacks and burns Heorot.
14. Beowulf resolves to fight the dragon and sets out with eleven attendants, guided by the runaway slave.
15. There is a hard fight and all the men run away except the loyal Wiglaf. Beowulf is slain, but he and Wiglaf kill the dragon and Wiglaf shows Beowulf the treasure before he dies. Beowulf thanks

the Ruler of All that he has been allowed to conquer, bids Wiglaf tell the Goth warriors to raise a mound to be seen from the sea, 'Beowulf's mound' and gives his armour to Wiglaf.

16. The Geats carry away the treasure to be placed within the mound. The dragon's corpse is pushed over the cliff. The funeral pyre. The building of the funeral mound.

Thus: A. Episodes 1, 2, 3, 4, 5, and 6 only could be chosen, and form an effective whole.
B. Episodes 7 and 8 form another section with 9 and 10 as an optional ending.
C. Episode 11 forms another section.
D. Episodes 12, 13, 14 and 15 form a further section, with 16 as an optional conclusion.

The teacher can select whichever section, A, B, C or D he feels appropriate for his class, or even attempt two sections with the older age group.

## Characterization and group work

A selection can be made from the following characters and/or character groups. Hrothgar; Wealhtheow; attendants on Hrothgar, including Wulfgar, Unferth, Wiglaf, Aeschere (i.e. possible contrasts of characters of these and other courtiers); Hygelac; Hygd; Heardred, attendants on Hygelac; Beowulf; Beowulf's companions/attendants; Grendel; Grendel's mother; Underwater beasts; Runaway slave; Dragon.

## Movement

Movement experience as part of the total drama experience is as important in this theme as in any other, but it is for the teacher to decide whether or not he wishes to begin with movement or with the language/literature side. If he decides to begin with movement, content such as the following could be introduced with the whole class, according to which episodes are to be developed in Drama.

Kingly processional and Ritual of life in Heorot with Hygelac, and later Beowulf, e.g. procedure with goblet
Building the hall (tree-felling, carrying, piling, etc.)
Grotesque, fierce (to be associated with Grendel, etc.)
Young heroic (to be associated with the young Beowulf)

Surreptitious, furtive (to be associated with the slave)
Festive activities of feastings, e.g. Acrobatics, dancing
Journeys across land and sea
Women's work making and arranging hangings, cleaning
Fights

If a hall is available for this work, here is a suggestion of one way it could be used for the action.

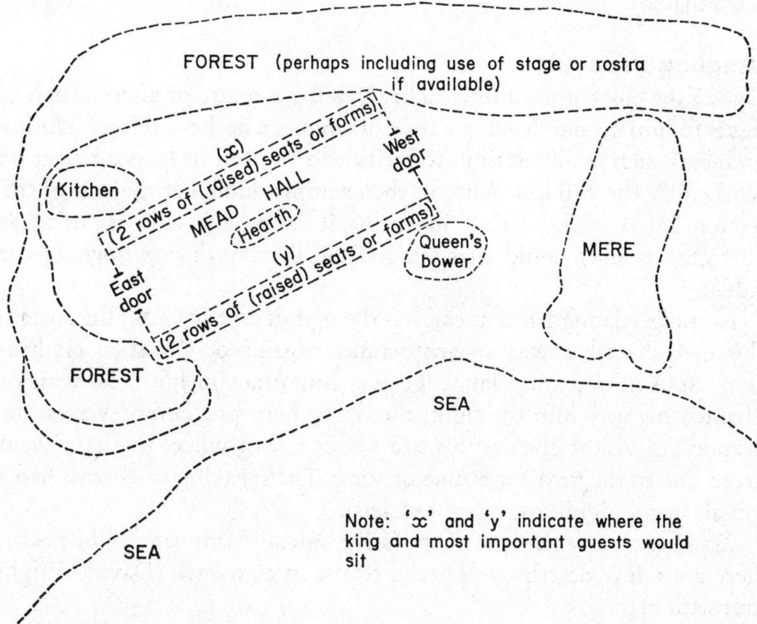


## Atmosphere building

Using language and movement, what are the possibilities of experiencing mood or dramatic atmosphere?

Pride in Heorot, confidence in the strength and government of Hrothgar
Heroic confidence of Beowulf and his men
Splendour of feastings
Fierce conflict of the fights

Slimy underwater battle in the mere

Doom brought (a) to Hrothgar by the monster Grendel and his mother (but at the time there was also the human evil of a feud in existence between Hrothgar's people and another tribe, the Heathobards).

(b) to the Geats by the Dragon (though there are reminders of quarrels between the Geats, Franks and Swedes. The suggestion is made that after Beowulf's death the Geats, through their misdeeds, will be anihilated).

## Language/speech

One of the chief aims of the teacher in using a centre of interest such as this is to initiate and develop a love of language in the children. The ingredients such as alliteration, sonority and rhythm of language can be relished by the children who, in the example quoted at the end of the section had a splendid time inventing it. They also enjoyed using as correctly as they could manage stylistic literary devices such as the riddle.

Although dating from as early as the eighth century A.D., the society this epic describes was an aristocratic, organized, Christian civilization. Spoken and sung language was important in life. The warrior chanted his way into the fight, the dying hero proclaimed verses, the wandering visitor chanted his story after a feast where the harp went from one to the next for a tune or song. The speaking of charms had a ritual, magic significance (see extracts).

There are many passages of evocative, splendid language in the poem; here are a few descriptive phrases to use in classwork (David Wright translation):

Hrothgar: 'generous king', 'of peaceful strength'.

Heorot: 'lofty and horn gabled', 'a handsome timbered hall, embellished with gold'.

Beowulf and statements by him: 'famed for his strong grip', 'steadfast', 'adventurer', 'stalwart, the strongest of living men', 'trusted Beowulf', 'I will grapple with the fiend with grip of hand and strive for life, foe against foe', 'of all kings the gentlest and most gracious of men'.

Beowulf's company of men and their armour: 'with clanging armour the Geats quickly leapt ashore', 'each tough, hand-rivited coat of mail sparkled and the shimmering rings of iron clinked in their armour', chainmail 'cunningly linked by skill of smith', 'my tough company of fighting men'.

Boat and sea journey (of the sea): 'swan's road'; (of the boat): 'the curved prow skimmed over the sea like a bird', 'foamy-necked floater', 'her timbers thrummed', 'the sea was crossed, the journey at an end'.

Grendel and his actions: 'mighty stalker of the marshes', 'grim demon', 'grim and greedy', 'dark death shadow', 'malign outcast', 'in the black night the prowler of the dark came stalking', 'the raging fiend with horrible firelit eyes', 'murderous pagan demon'.

Grendel's mother: she was one of the creatures that were forced to live in the icy currents of abominable lakes, 'grisly guardian of the abyss', 'she made a lunge and grabbed the hero with her loathsome claws'.

Dragon: 'scaly, malicious Worm', 'it slid implacably over the rocks'.

Examples of action and sounds: 'a great cry went up in the morning', 'the hall thundered with hubbub', 'raging, beserk, in despair of life, he swung its whorled blade and furiously struck', 'his battlecry thundered under the grey rock'.

Examples of scenery: 'an unvisited land among wolf-haunted hill, windswept crags, and perilous fen-tracks, where mountain waterfalls disappear into mists and are lost underground', 'the lake . . . . overhung with graves of rime-crusted trees whose thick roots darken the water', 'strange dragons groping in the depths'.

## Historical and literary sources

These can be made use of to extend the understanding of the children and to stimulate their creative work in speech, writing, craft and movement. 'Beowulf' states much about the Anglo-Saxon outlook and imagination, and the text is rich in suitable extracts. However, additional background sources can be found, such as the following.

## Extracts from various sources

A. *Attitude to the chief lord: duties of thanes, King and Queen; law; battle*

1. Tacitus, *Germania*

Furthermore it is a lifelong infamy and reproach to survive the chief and withdraw from battle. To defend him, to protect him, even to ascribe to his glory their own exploits, is the essence of their sworn allegiance. The chiefs fight for victory, the followers for their chief.

2. Old Norse poem, *Havanaal* (being the moral principles guiding the age)
Wisdom and foresight must be the guiding stars of life. The son of the chief must be silent, reflecting and grave in all battles, gay and generous towards all until the hour of death. Let no one be without arms for he cannot know if he will have need of them on his journey . . . . The fool believes that he can live always if he avoids a fight, but old age does not recompense as the sword. Rich and poor succumb alike but an illustrious name never perishes . . . Richness is as the twinkling of an eye, it is the most inconstant of friends. A great intelligence is the best provision for it is the resource of the oppressed. One must not be too well informed and one must not know one's destiny beforehand, if one is to be free of preoccupations . . . If you have a friend who possesses your confidence mix your thoughts with him, exchange presents and visit him often. Be good to the unfortunate for their prayers will bring you happiness. Never mock a speaker with white hair; it is often good to listen to what old men say, and good words often come out of the mouth of a wrinkled old man. The son of man carries on his breast a mixture of vice and virtue – no one is so perfect that he is without fault nor so evil that he is worth nothing.

3. Scandinavian Law (extract)
An assembly is to be held and the twelve leading thanes are to go out and swear on the relics that they will accuse not guiltless man nor conceal any guilty one and they are to arrest the man frequently accused.

4. Early Christian Oath of Allegiance to the lord
By the lord, before whom these relics are holy, I will be loyal and true to . . . . . . . . . . ., and love all that he loves, and hate all that he hates, however in accordance with God's rights and secular obligations; and never, willingly and intentionally, in word or deed, do anything that is hateful to him; on condition that he shall keep me as I shall deserve, and carry out all that was our agreement, when I subjected myself to him and chose his favour.

5. 'The Wanderer', a poem (extract). A lament for a dead lord

All joy has departed. Truly does he know this who must long forgo the advice of his dear lord. When sorrow and sleep both together often bind the wretched lonely man, it seems to him in his mind that he embraces and kisses his liege lord, and lays hands and head on his knee, as sometimes in the days of yore he enjoyed the bounty from the throne. Then awakens the friendless man; he sees before him the dark waves, the sea birds dipping, spreading their wings, frost and snow falling, mingled with hail. Then are the wounds of his heart the heavier, the sore wounds after his dear one; his sorrow is renewed.

6. Extracts from *The Battle of Maldon*

(a) Quickly was Offa cut down in the fight; yet he had carried out what he had promised his lord, when he vowed to his treasure giver that both together they should ride safely home into the stronghold, or fall in the army, die of wounds on the field of battle. He lay as befits a thane, close by his lord.

(b) Byrhnoth bade men leave their horses, let them go and turn to warfare, think on strength and good courage. Offa's kinsmen found Byrhnoth would bear no faint-heartedness so he let his well-loved hawk fly away from his hand to the wood and strode to the battle. . . . . Then Byrhnoth began to put his men in array; he rode about and gave rede, he showed his warriors how they should stand and keep the field and bade them hold their spears aright fast in their hands and fear nothing. Then he alighted amid his people, where it most pleased him, where his most faithful heart companions were.

7. Gnomic verses from *English Literature from the Beginning to the Norman Conquest*, S. A. Brooke

(a) A king shall with cattle, with armlets and beakers
Purchase his queen . . . . the spirit of battle
Shall grow in the man, but the woman shall thrive
Beloved in her people, shall cheerfully live.
Counsel shall keep, shall large hearted be
With horses and treasure and at giving of mead;
Everywhere always she shall earliest greet
The prince of the nobles before his retainers:
To the hand of her lord the first cup of all
Straightway she shall give,

(b) He the king shall hold the kingdom.
Cities shall afar be seen.
Those that are upon this earth, artful work of giants,
Wondrous work of wall stones! Wind in air is swiftest,
Thunder on its path the loudest. Mighty are the powers of Christ!
Wyrd is strongest! Winter coldest
Most hoar frosts has Spring, its cold the longest!
Summer is sun lovliest, then the sky is hottest.
Autumn above all is glorious, unto men it brings
All the graining of the year God doth send to them.

B. *Ships and Life at sea*

1. Tacitus, *Germania*

They have mighty fleets. The shape of their ships is different, in that having prow at each end, they are always ready for running on to the beach. They are not worked by sails, nor are the oars fastened to the sides in regular order, but let loose as in some rivers, so that they can be shifted here or there as circumstances may require.

2. Caesar, describing the Vebiti of Brittany

The prows were very much elevated as also the stern so as to encounter heavy waves and storms.

3. Saxon sailors by Sidonius, Gallo Roman noble, latter half of the fifth century

When you see the rowers of that nation, you may at once make up your mind that every one of them is an arch pirate; with such wonderful unanimity do all at once command, obey, teach and learn their one chosen business of brigandage. For this reason I ought to warn you to be more than ever on your guard in this warfare. Your enemy is the most ferocious of all enemies. Unexpectedly he attacks; when he escapes he despises those who block his path, he overthrows those who are off their guard, he always succeeds in cutting off the enemy whom he follows, while he never fails when he desires to effect his own escape. .... The dangers of the deep are to them not casual acquaintances but intimate friends, for since a tempest throws the invaded off their guard and prevents the invaders from being descried from afar, they hail with joy the crash of waves on the rocks which gives them their best chance of escaping from other enemies than the elements. ... before they set sail from the continent to their own country, their custom is to collect the crowd of their prisoners together, by a mockery of equity make them cast lots which of them shall undergo the iniquitous sentence of death, and then at the moment of departure to abandon every tenth captive to the slow agony of a watery end, a practice which is the most lamentable because it arises from a superstitious notion that they will thus ensure for themselves a safe return.

C. *Charms*

1. Charm: on departing on a journey

In this rod I guard myself and to God's grace trust myself
Gainst the stitch that sore is and against the sore blow
And against the grim, against the grisly terror,
And against the mickle horror to everyone is loathly.
And against all the loathly things that into the land may come.
A victorious spell I sing, a victorious staff I bear,
Word of victory, work of victory, so may this avail me!
May no spirit harm me nor the mighty man afflict me.

2. Farmer's Charm, pre-Norman Conquest
(The farmer takes meal, kneads it with milk and lays it under a furrow)

Acre, full fed, bring forth fodder for men!
Blossoming brightly, blessed become!
And the god who wrought with earth grant us gift of growing.

(And he then drives the plough on)

D. *Riddles.*

(a) I went from home
I travelled from home
I looked on the road of roads.
Road was above,
Road was beneath
And road in every direction.

*Answer*
A bird flew above
A fish swam beneath
You walked on a bridge.

(b) What kind of drink was it
I drank yesterday?
It was neither water nor wine
Mead nor ale
No kind of food.
However I went thirstless thence.

*Answer*
You went into the sunshine
Hid yourself in the shade;
There fell dew in the valleys;
Then you did taste
The night dew
Cooling the throat by it.

(c) What wonder is it
I saw outside
Before the doors of Delling?
It turns its head
On the way to hell
And its feet to the sun.

*Answer*
The head of the leek turns
towards the heart of the earth
And its leaves into the air.

(d) A storm riddle

Who so wary and so wise of the warriors lives
That he dare declare who doth drive me on my way.
When I start up in my strength! Oft in stormy wrath,
Hugely then I thunder, tear along in gusts,
Far above the floor of the earth, burn the folk halls down
Ravage all the rooms! Great on earth the din
And slaughter qualm of men. Then I shake the world,
Forests rich in fruit. Say who shuts me in
Or what is my name I who bear this burden.

(e) From the *Herwarar Saga*

What beast is that
Which defends the Danes?
It has a bloody back
And shelters men,
Meets the weapons,

Exposes its life,
Man lays his body
Against its palm.

*Answer*
The shields shine
In the battles
And protect those who wield them.

(f) Who lives on high mountains
Who lives in deep dales
Who lives without breath
Who is never silent?

*Answer*
Ravens live on high mountains
Dew falls in deep dales
Fish live without breath in water
But the sounding waterfall
Is never silent.

E. *Miscellaneous poetic extracts*

1. Rune song

Ice is overcold, immeasurably slippy,
It glistens bright as glass, unto gems most like,
'Tis a floor frost wrought, fair unto the sight.

2. Gnomic verse: ruins

Wondrous is this wall of stone; Wyrds[1] have shattered it!
Broken are the burg-steads, crumbled down the giant's work!
Fallen are the roof beams, ruined are the towers.
All undone the door-pierced turrets; frozen dew is on their plaster.
Shorn away and sunken down, are the sheltering battlements,
Under-eaten with old age. Steep the court that fell,
Brilliant were the burg-steads, burn-fed houses many
High the heap of horned gables, of the host a mickle sound
Many were the mead halls, full of mirth of men
Till the strong-walled Wyrd willed that all to change
In a slaughter wide they fell, woeful days of bale came on;
Famine death took fortitude from men!
All their battle bulwarks bared to their foundations are;
Crumbled is the castle keep.

[1] Wyrds: possibly Weirds, or Fate/fortune

It is clear that certain characteristics of life in Anglo Saxon times can be appreciated from extracts such as these. Ideas for characterization (the attitude of characters and the values they hold) together with ideas for movement, incidents and occupations within the action are thus stimulated.

The historical elements in *Beowulf* give the story greater significance. It interests children to know that the site of Hrothgar's palace of Heorot has been identified with the village of Leire on the Danish island Seeland. The sixth-century feuds and wars of the Geats, Danes and Swedes were well known in the eighth century. However Beowulf, Grendel and the Dragon belong to the mythical element of the story. Questions about Christianity are usually asked by the children, and the teacher must be ready for these. *Beowulf* contains a mixture of Christian and heathen attitudes. Christianity came to England in A.D. 597 but certain heathen customs continued, for instance, a priest had to observe certain taboos: he was not allowed to carry weapons or to ride on anything but a mare. He was believed to be able to bind his enemies' hands by chanting spells from a high mound. There was a trust in incantations and amulets. The oath of allegiance continued to imply rights of vengeance in spite of the sanctity bestowed on the oath by the Christian Church. (See book list for further help on life of the times.)

Individual reading cards can be provided with questions and/or suggestions for further work, such as:

1. Picture/description of horns.
2. Picture/description Queen Wealhtheow with cup.
3. Picture/description of armour.
4. Description of Viking ship.
5. Description of money used – ring money, gold.
6. Viking names for swords: (the children can make up names for their own swords) e.g. 'The gleam of battle', 'The battle snake', 'The glow of war', 'The fire of the battle', 'The fire of the sea kings'.
7. Extracts from *Beowulf* to read and then explain the meaning of underlined words: e.g. description of Grendel, description

of procedure in Heorot, description of Heorot, description of presents.

### Art and Craft

Examples of earlier Anglo Saxon wealth and magnificance can be seen in the exhibition and illustrations available of the Sutton Hoo archaeological finds at the British Museum, London. These are a useful basis for art and craft work in connection with *Beowulf* centre of interest. Especially worth studying are the sword, shield, helmet, battle standard, golden harness with carved belt-buckle, harp and ceremonial drinking horns.

Armour can be made from cardboard and painted, and/or embossed with rope. Each thane should have his own shield, helmet and named sword or lance. Each lady should have long thick string plaits, 'jewels' and simple tunics painted with suitable designs.

If further craft work is wished for, the monsters and underwater creatures can have masks and/or even simple costumes painted with scales and other likely monster motives. Large background murals depicting the scenes could be made: such as the forest, the mere, the kitchen, the queen's bower, Heorot, the sea cliffs.

### Music

Attempts should be made to play the children some music of the correct period.

Perhaps even more important than this is to interest the children in making their own accompaniment for parts of the drama, and to enjoy it as much as Hrothgar's court did, music being an important part of life. The instruments used should be as historically suitable as possible, e.g. psaltery, harp, pipe, drum, guitar. Nobles could play the harp and sing; to prevent slaves from pretending to be gentlemen they were forbidden to play the harp.

However this aim of authenticity, as far as possible, should be concerned with interesting the children in subject matter, and should not be done in a way that impedes progress of their own creative work. Anything they do in this context is welcomed, for instance, in the example of the children's work quoted, the use of the folksong and *Greensleeves* was their own very best effort, and as such highly commended. But the teacher can make good use of opportunities for suggesting appropriate music when his advice is sought, when he feels a suggestion will not stultify the children's spontaneity and during a definite class teaching period.

In some literary/historical legendary folk themes it is allowable to use modern music as accompaniment: sometimes a modern composer can be found who has written well in the style, or as a result of having been inspired by the style. For example, Benjamin Britten in *A Ceremony of Carols* (medieval-Tudor inspiration); Carl Orff, *Carmina Burana* (medieval inspiration). This music may be found more stimulating and suitable for classwork than the historically authentic pieces though if sufficiently interesting authentic pieces can be found suitable for dramatic movement accompaniment, they should be used. In working on this theme of *Beowulf*, since some of the value lies in the literary/historical sphere, it would be a pity to work against this by using inappropriate music. Silence, spoken word or simple percussion accompaniment or sound effects would be preferable to modern music.

## THE EPIC OF BEOWULF AND GRENDEL BY A GROUP OF NINE TO TEN-YEAR-OLDS

The following play was written by a group of nine to ten-year-olds during work around *Beowulf*. It is not quoted as an example of the most excellent work that can be achieved, but merits inclusion in that it is the work of an average group of children with mainly very limited home background. The results, such as they are, were entirely stimulated by the material the teacher introduced: her selection of apt, vivid passages from *Beowulf*, her use of background source quotations as mentioned on page 133 and work in movement. The play was written from a tape recording of their final 'performance'. It is interesting to note how the children have managed to absorb something of the rhythm and style of the original, and yet it reveals other experience too, for instance we have Beowulf's men chanting a well-known sea shanty, 'The St. Ives Riddle', and the use of the tune *Greensleeves* recently learnt in a different, more appropriate context.

NARRATOR: The minstrels take the song of the wickedness of Grendel to Hygelac's realm where a brave warrior called Beowulf lives.

(*Minstrel's song. Child's own tune.*)

MINSTREL: There be a monster name is Grendel,
He is eating up the people,
When they go to have a ball,
In the high and lofty mead hall.
The Queen was sitting on the throne,
When she heard old Grendel's moan,
All the men were fast asleep,
So they couldn't hear Grendel creep
Through the door and in the hall,
Creeping up to the Gift stool.
Now he did eat up all the people,
When they went to have a ball
In the high and lofty mead hall.
Now if ye will, all ye people,
Go and rid them of this evil,
Bring them happiness for life,
Rid them of this desperate strife.

HYGELAC: Beowulf, if what the minstrels sing is true, this
Should be a good mission for you.

BEOWULF: O gracious sire, I will sail to Hrothgar's realm to help rid them of this terrible monster from the deep and slimy mere.

NARRATOR: Beowulf and his men went down to the shore. (*They prepare the ship.*) They set sail and were soon in Hrothgar's realm. (*They embark.*)

MEN: Way haul away, we'll haul away the bowline (*folk-song tune.*)
Way haul away, we'll haul away Joe
Way haul away, the packet is a-rolling
Way haul away, we'll haul away Joe.

COASTGUARD: Who are ye who come here dressed for war?

BEOWULF: My name is Beowulf. I am come to help King Hrothgar get rid of the mighty stalker Grendel.

COASTGUARD: Then come in haste and follow me. I will get an audience with the King with you.

NARRATOR: The coastguard goes to get an audience with the King. (*March.*)

COASTGUARD: O gracious sire, there are some warriors who wish an audience with you.

NARRATOR: The King sat silent.

COASTGUARD: The leader says his name is Beowulf.

HROTHGAR: Why, I knew him as a lad! Bring him in.

COASTGUARD: The King will see you now.

NARRATOR: The King and Beowulf make plans. Then that night they all went to the mead hall. At the mead hall the Queen is handing round a goblet.

QUEEN: Drink of this, ye great warriors, tonight ye can be glad.

NARRATOR: The Queen gets to Beowulf.

QUEEN: I hope the wine is good.

BEOWULF: The wine is very good, my lady. How about some music?

NARRATOR: The minstrel gets up and sings. (*Tune – Greensleeves.*)

MINSTREL: There was a knight of early days
Who would go anywhere to get a fight with another knight –
A jolly brave knight was he.
He picked a fight with another knight
His opponent there was strong
His opponent lived to tell the tale
And to be able to sing this song.
These knights they fight from left to right,
These knights were bold and fierce,
The knight wished to fight with the other knight
Got a blow right on his head and he fell down dead,
And he fell, down, dead.

NARRATOR: The warrior tells a riddle.

WARRIOR: As I was coming to the mead hall, I met a man with seven wives. Each wife had seven sacks, each sack had seven cats, each cat had seven kits. Kits, cats, sacks and wives, how many were coming to the mead hall?

ANSWER: One was going.

NARRATOR: Everyone was puzzled. Then King Hrothgar said.

KING: Come it is time for us to go.

NARRATOR: The night of the fight everyone was asleep except the guard. Grendel came creeping. (*Noise, including remarks such as* 'What's that?' 'It must be Grendel'.) The fight begins. (*Noise.*)

VOICE: Surely he will be killed!

NARRATOR: The fight goes on until Beowulf wrenches off Grendel's right arm, Grendel fights back in terror, but he is defeated. He makes one mad rush for the door and stalks back to his marsh.

KING: Well done Beowulf.

NARRATOR: The King comes rushing in.

KING; Is Grendel dead?

BEOWULF: No I should have held on longer.

KING: Don't worry ye did well.

NARRATOR: Next day people came from far and wide to see the arm of Grendel and to see the traces of the monster. Beowulf was a hero.

KING: Beowulf, will you stay and be my guest?

BEOWULF: I shall be honoured.

NARRATOR: After a few days, Beowulf and his men left. (*They prepare the ship and embark.*) That is the end of our play.

*Excerpts from minstrel's songs for another play of Beowulf by children aged 9–10*

O listen Hygelac's realm, to the story of
  Grendel, monster of the deep,
Who comes at night to the Mead Hall, and
  Kills warriors asleep.
He lives in marshes, mud and slime,
He hates the song of dog and lion.
O help us please, dear Hygelac's realm,
To bring this dog of devils down.

There is a treacherous monster from the
  Deep, deep, deep,
The thing that he likes doing best is to
  Eat, eat, eat,
But the thing that he doth eat
Is a very weird thing,
For the things that he doth eat
Are people, dead and neat.
He takes them to his cave
To eat them in his leisure,
But I don't see how he's getting any pleasure.

He crept about, the monster,
In his home, the sloshy marsh.
One day he went a-creeping
To the Great Hall, the Mead,
He stabbed a man who was sleeping,
And hurried off with speed.
The next day he killed thirty,
And methinks that's very dirty,
And we all hope
That monstrous dope
Does not come to our land
And does not come to us; pom, pom.

BOOK LIST

Study of a selection of the following will be found helpful to the teacher in preparation for work on Beowulf:

Dorothy Whitelock, *The Beginnings of English Society (Anglo Saxon Period)*, Penguin Books
*The Anglo Saxon Chronicle*, trans. G. N. Garmonsway, Everyman
Marjorie and C. H. B. Quennell, *Everyday Life in Anglo Saxon, Viking and Norman Times*, Batsford
T. C. Lethbridge, *Merlin's Island*, Routledge & Kegan Paul
*Anglo Saxon England*, BBC Publications
F. M. Stenton, *Anglo Saxon England*, Oxford University Press
R. H. Hodgkin, *A History of the Anglo Saxons*, 3rd ed. Oxford University Press.
H. M. Chadwick, *Studies in Anglo Saxon Institutions*, Cambridge University Press
R. W. Chambers, *England Before the Norman Conquest*, Longmans
R. L. S. Bruce Mitford, *The Sutton Hoo Ship Burial*, British Museum Publications, 1947
Helen Wadell, *The Wandering Scholars*, Constable
*The Early Middle Ages*, ed. R. H. C. Davis (English History in Pictures series), Routledge & Kegan Paul
E. T. Leeds, *Anglo Saxon Art and Archaeology*, Oxford University Press
T. D. Kendrick, *Anglo Saxon Art*, Methuen
T. D. Kendrick, *Late Saxon and Viking Art*, Methuen
D. Talbot Rice, *English Art 871–1100*, Oxford University Press
W. P. Ker, *Epic and Romance*, Constable
W. P. Ker, *English Literature, Medieval*, Williams & Norgate
S. A. Brooke, *English Literature to the Norman Conquest*, Macmillan
R. K. Gordon, *Anglo Saxon Poetry*, Everyman
*Old Norse Sagas and Legends*
K. F. Boult, *Asgard and Norse Heroes*, Dent

B. S. Phillpotts, *Edda and Saga*, Thornton & Butterworth
Axel Olrik, *Heroic Legends of Denmark*, American-Scandinavian Foundation, N.Y.
*Early Medieval Music*, New Oxford History
O. Jesperson, *Growth and Structure of the English Language*, Blackwell
H. Sweet, *An Anglo-Saxon Primer*, Oxford University Press
W. W. Lawrence, *Beowulf and the Epic Tradition*, Hafner
Dorothy Whitelock, *The Audience of Beowulf*, Oxford University Press
R. W. Chambers, *Introduction to Beowulf*, Cambridge University Press
*Beowulf*, trans. by Huyshe; Ian Serraillier; C. L. Thomson; Clark Hall (Revised Wrenn, 1950): David Wright (Penguin Books).

## ENERGY

Drama can be introduced, or arise, during work on various aspects of this theme such as the use of muscles, animals, the wheel, wind, water, coal and steam.

### 1. The Beginning

The story of the famous discovery of steam by Hero of Alexandria, 2000 years ago, is told.

The scene can be dramatized, showing the 'magic' opening of the doors in the Temple, as it would appear to a group of people at the time, with dance and music accompaniment.

The teacher can then discuss with the class the secret of the opening of the doors, explaining that long centuries would pass before the immense potentialities of steam were realized.

### 2. Relation of Muscles to Energy

Class discussion on man's use of his own muscles throughout history can follow, introducing his need of implements. No doubt many examples will be suggested by the children, some of which can be dramatized. Here are a few suggestions:

*Women at the well.* Emphasis is needed on the actual muscular effort. The conversation at the well can reveal the dependence of man through centuries on this human effort. Famous stories of people meeting at the well may be used.

*The work of Slaves.* Many examples can be found of this tragic aspect of man's history; building of Pyramids, galley slaves, etc. Some of the reasons may be considered – the need for human muscular work: in Africa, the special problem arising because of the ravages of the tsetse fly in killing animals useful for transport. Actual stories of slaves at work can be used.

*Man with implements.* Again many examples can be found. Perhaps pictures such as Van Gogh, 'Peasant reaping corn' or Pieter Bruegel the Elder, 'The Harvesters' can be starting points. But it is of course not necessary to take examples from the past. Everyday scenes, familiar to the children, in which tools are used, can be improvised.

The children might even take school cleaning and the stoking of the boilers. Next there could be an introduction to Man's use of the muscular power of animals. Class discussion will soon show the importance of the horse, donkey, ox, yak, camel. . . .

Among the numberless dramatic scenes that might be chosen, here is an unusual story which can be the basis of scenes involving group action, and one which shows an incident where man is totally dependent on an animal for his life. It occurs in the biography of Lassiter, *Lassiter's last ride*.

The outline of the story is as follows: Lassiter is searching for gold in the Western Desert of Australia. He loses contact with the rest of the party, is allowed to travel with a group of Aboriginal nomads, seeking food. When they fail to find it, the leaders decide that the white man is putting 'bad magic' on them. They 'point the finger' at him and intend to kill him. An old man of the tribe tries to befriend him. He is left alone with a little food and his camel. One day the camel runs away. Alone and helpless, he dies. He had scrawled on a piece of paper found later, 'A reef of gold! . . . . I would give it all for a loaf of bread'.

*Suggested scenes*

1. *A meeting of the Tribe*

This can begin with a meeting of the chief men. The women are apart with the children. Lassiter is seated on a stone looking into the distance. The chief men talk of tribal affairs, decide they must move on. One of them shows dislike of 'the white man'. Feeling builds up against him. He is thought to be the reason for their failure to find food. The old man tries to defend him. It is decided to 'point the finger' at him.

2. *The Ceremony*
All the tribe are gathered together. A tribal dance is followed by the evil, antagonistic 'pointing finger' action. Strange words and songs used.

Later, secretly, the old man brings Lassiter some food.

Lassiter, now alone, awakens one morning, in a cave, to find the camel gone. He cries out, searches, talks to himself about the horror of being lost in the desert.

No doubt in class discussion, more lighthearted stories about man and his animal helpers will be found, and can be used for dramatic work.

## 3. Man, Animals and the Wheel

The immense importance of the invention of the wheel in the development of man's life will be stressed.

*Suggestions.* A 'Covered Wagon' scene. The history of North America and South Africa of course, are rich in all kinds of stories, where the covered wagon trail is at the heart of the people's experiences. No doubt the children will hardly need prompting to improvise scenes with American setting.

Here is a covered wagon story, with a difference, taken from the history of South Africa, with dramatic possibilities.

*The Background*
In 1835, after the abolition by the British Government of slavery in all its territories, the Boer (Dutch) farmers began the 'Great Trek' away from the Cape Town area. Using covered wagons piled with goods and family treasures, groups moved with their animals across the plateau eastwards, in search of pasture land where they could settle, far away from an 'interfering' government. To their astonishment they met Africans far more powerful than those they had enslaved in the Cape area: moreover, these Africans were seeking pasture too. Violent clashes were inevitable. Frequently it took the following form: the Boers sent out scouts on horseback to see any signs of African attack. If danger threatened, they made a temporary encampment, protected by a square-shaped wall formed by their wagons, reinforced by piles of thornbush. The Africans could throw their spears with deadly effect, but the Boers had guns. As so often happened elsewhere, the men with

the guns were eventually victorious, and as one writer comments, 'the back of the African was broken' (with consequences recognizable today).

*Suggestions for scene*

Scouts have returned; they report an attack is likely. Everyone knows what has to be done; one man directs; with speed the protecting wall is made. The children and old people are placed in protected positions. Men with guns watch for the first signs of attack, give the warning. They are not visible to the attackers. The Africans attack, and some of the Boers are killed or wounded. But the firing guns drive away the invaders. (Various scenes, if desired, could be improvised, for groups of children.)

## 4. Man's Attempts to Tame Wind and Water

No attempt is made here to deal with this as a whole subject. The intention is simply to use it as transition to the coming of steam.

(a) As introductory background, the teacher may like to use ideas from an early English play, *The Play of the Weather* for a dramatic representation of the possible conflict between people whose livelihood depends on the sympathetic behaviour of the elements. The children can be encouraged to think further on this subject, make up their own dialogues or even short plays on this theme.

(b) A scene takes place at an Inn in a Yorkshire village in the early nineteenth century. A group of local people are chatting. Local gossip and the weather are, of course, the main topics. Mention may be made of the War with France, but weather is soon in the picture again (partly because good weather for one kind of work, is the opposite for another). Two of the men present have windmills on their land, another a waterwheel. A local farmer rejoices in the spell of calm bright weather, but the windmill owner grumbles. Then two of the women lead the talk. One of them mentions a letter from a brother. She gives family news, then says that there is trouble in her brother's village because a factory using a steam engine has been built. A young man raises the question of using steam power to grind corn. The windmill owner scorns the idea, but obviously, is disturbed at the signs of change.

## 5. Coal and steam

Introduction: A short extract from Marco Polo's writings can be read, in which he mentions that the people of Cathay burn 'black stones'.[22]

The use of coal in Britain for heating before the age of steam can be explained.

*Suggested scenes*

'Long ago in ancient China'

Marco Polo is in a house in Cathay. It is winter with bitter N.W. winds. He talks with the family; asks questions about clothing in winter, food, etc.

Later that evening he writes in his diary the strange tale of the black stones, noting that they are still glowing in the morning.

Brief explanation of the origin of coal should be given.

Explanation given of the first use of steam in the pumping of water from mines. The story of James Watt is briefly told.[23]

The teacher may like to take the children to a Science Museum (as in London or Birmingham), and then ask the children to answer the question, 'What was James Watts' Great Discovery?'

The victory of steam can then be described in pits, factories, for railways and ships: in association with iron. (Each one of these can be used as a Centre of Interest with many dramatic possibilities.)

Discussion with the children on 'Who lost the Battle?'

*Revolt of the Handloom Weavers*

The story which will serve as a basis for older children can either be taken from Mrs Gaskell's *Life of Charlotte Brontë*[24] or from the novel *Shirley* by Charlotte Brontë[25].

*Coal in 1969*

Discussion with the class may suggest that coal is now losing the battle. Partly to correct this, the children could be taken to the local Power Station and discover for themselves that Coal and Steam still serve our lives – in our coal – electric power stations and of course in other ways.

## IDEAS FROM THE SKY

### 'Movement' of the Sun

Over a period of time the children are asked to observe the position of the Sun in the sky, and its 'movements' at different times of the day, to make drawings and keep records. Class conversation follows. Attention is called to: 'Man's interest in the Sun at all times in his history'. Children express their own feelings about the Sun.

Examples are taken to show man's attitude to the Sun. Festivals of different periods may be used:

(i) The Inca Festival of the Sun.
(ii) The Swedish candle-light festival to welcome the end of winter.
(iii) The Midnight Sun in N. Norway in December.

(iii) would probably be the simplest to prepare. The scene could take place on the mountains. Young people sing and dance. It is a cloudy night; They are waiting for the clouds to clear as the village church clock below, faintly chimes midnight. At last the Sun appears, low on the horizon but visible. They sing and dance again, then gather round the fire. Some of them relate stories with lively responses from the rest.

The children are asked to say what they think happens to the Sun when wecannot see it. Then they are told what some people of ancient times believed.[26]

### Now comes the Galileo story

It is suggested that the teacher may like to 'make use of' Brecht's impressive play, *Galileo*.[27] How this is done, naturally depends on the age of the children. Parts of the play can be read by the teacher, or better still, if copies are available, older children may read it together. The readings in any case should follow the children's own dramatic enterprises. The following suggested scenes are directly based on the play, and of course the children are told this.

The teacher briefly outlines the scene in which Galileo teaches Andreas, young son of his housekeeper, about the new idea, that the Earth travels round the Sun! The housekeeper and Galileo's daughter are briefly described, and their attitude to the new idea.

The children now discuss the 'new idea', and the period when it was first expressed. They can give their own views on it. A scene may then be worked out, the children inventing a way for Galileo to explain it to the ten-year-old boy. Some of them may wish to display disbelief like the housekeeper.

Then follows a reading from the play in which Galileo shows to Andreas in a practical way, the 'movement'.[28] The teacher tells the children of the disbelief and anger the new idea evoked, and the ways in which these attitudes were expressed in the market place, where learned men were gathered together to discuss the new doctrine, in the course of which torture was mentioned as a means of silencing Galileo.

*The Market Place*

Galileo is made fun of by the people. The children can be encouraged to make up verses, even songs, of derision. Others may invent a clowning act – or draw pictures – e.g. Galileo falling off the earth as it rushes on. Opportunity can be given for the usual market business.

The market scene by Brecht may then be read.[29] The class is told that many years pass, Andreas is a young man now. Galileo has been arrested and ordered to recant. Rumour says he has been threatened with torture. The day comes when Galileo must decide.

*Again in the Market Place. The Recantation*

The class can discuss how they will dramatize this. They are told the bell will ring, the words of recantation will be heard, and that, in the play, Andreas has been waiting in intense excitement, certain that his great Master will never go back on the truths he has found.

The scene in the play is then read, where Andreas scorns his former teacher and Galileo replies.[30]

Galileo, alone, after years of house arrest. The meeting between Galileo and his former pupil can be described. Andreas discovers two things:

(i) That Galileo has continued his scientific work, and secretly by candle-light at night made a copy, though nearly blind. He asks Andreas to smuggle it out for the world to read some day.
(ii) That Galileo now grieves that he failed in not standing by the truth he knew.[31]

### Out into Space

Space or space travel is a popular and important contemporary theme but it needs to be tackled in a thorough manner with thought given to problems of scientific exploration. It should be made clear when a factual and when a fantasy interpretation of events is being experienced. Drama material from the subject also includes stories of the stars in myth and legend and how they were named; uses of the stars through history, by Babylonians, Assyrians, Egyptians; Stonehenge; by Incas, Mayas and Greeks. Stars in the Bible, stories of dreams and soothsayers. Junior age children are quick to invent fantasy creatures from outer space and art, craft, music and written work are natural adjuncts to drama for this theme. For a simple dramatic representation of the arrival of news from a new world discovered in the moon, see Ben Jonson's masque of that name. This would definitely not be suitable for children's use, but is of interest as background material for the teacher. According to the herald in Jonson's masque, life is delightful in the moon, coaches and boats are made of clouds and clouds can be bought for the protection of invisibility. And 'all the Phantasticall creatures you can think of are there including part men part birds that hop from island to island.'

## A TOPICAL EVENT

Machines of all sorts, including robots, are popular in Junior school drama. Now follows a description (written for me by their class teacher), of a machine play made up by a class of eleven to twelve-year-old boys, showing how a topical event can sometimes lead to drama. The idea here arose from class work with decimal currency and from the discussion which followed this.

The 'machines' were composed of five groups of boys. The groups decided on their own movement and noise, using a common pulse but regular and irregular rhythms. Two examples of the kind of movement they were inventing with suggestions for development:

*Machine A*

Boys stood elbows tucked in sides, forearms at right angles. Moved slowly from side to side, right foot crossing in front of left foot, and then back again. The noise (mmm, mmm,) accentuated each time the foot hit the ground.

*Machine B*

Boys knelt in pairs, facing each other, arms outstretched and meeting at a central point. Then, keeping arms straight, leaning body and arms away from opposite pair, and then coming back to the same position. A hissing noise.

These boys had not had any movement/drama experience, hence the limited movement content. Following opportunities for exploratory work, stimulated by the teacher's suggestions, further development might be: machine A – changes of level, crouching on haunches for recharge of pistons, then shooting up high. Changes of direction (i.e. where facing) could be introduced, e.g. a sudden body twist to the back, or leaning over sideways). More use could be made of arms, perhaps dynamic accents, inward, downward, backward, or upward. Another sound such as 'cha' could be made.

Machine B might introduce repetitive jerking movements of elbows, shoulders. After work on the leaning possibilities of the body while kneeling perhaps the children would introduce something like a long sustained pulling movement travelling successively along the line during the second part of their phrase. A $\frac{9}{4}$ rhythm could evolve naturally from this:

## Brief outline of the play

Machine groups in crouched position and still, so that they do not interfere by taking away attention from opening action. One boy warns audience about the lights and the bell effects to come, and then introduces Professor and assistant to audience.

Professor talks to the audience as though they had specifically come to listen to him and to watch the coming demonstration, thus making them in some small way actor participants. He talks about Decimal Day, and his machines which make the New Pence and how the audience will be the first to see the new coins made. The first machine is turned on, which slowly rises from its crouching starting position and begins its movement and noise. Having been given sufficient time to demonstrate, the volume is then turned down, and the machine continues its movement without noise. The next machine is then turned on, and performs its movement and noise, and then its volume is turned down. This is repeated until all machines are working, the last machine making no noise at all, so that the chink as it drops its coins into a metal box, can be clearly heard. Then volume is turned up so that all machines can be heard together.

The master control is then switched off, the volume dies as the machines return to original positions. The Professor then addresses audience and asks if there are any questions. A boy at the back points to two boys and asks what they do as they have not yet moved. He is told they are robots who guard the money. The Professor then says that as there are no more questions he will now leave. He thanks them and asks assistant to switch off the lights.

As soon as the lights are off two boys at the back of the hall switch on torches and one addressing the other suggests that they make some money for themselves. When on stage, one of them switches lights back on, and then remembers the robots, and voices fears that they will be caught and put in prison for stealing. The other, braver, dismisses this idea and advances cautiously on the robots. When no movement is made by them he becomes more confident, and finally gives each robot a small push to show his friend that they are lifeless.

They then work the machines, again one at a time, but this time in fairly quick succession and leaving the volume on all the time. They watch the money being made, but then one becomes impatient. He switches the machines off and they again return to original positions. The boy explains how he wants the money to come out faster, and hits on the idea of turning the volume full up. All the machines start up together, at first work correctly, but then jog each other and begin to run wild. Hastily the machines are turned off. The boys decide there is enough money anyway. As they try to lift the box the two robots move either side of them, lift arms and join hands together, and then allow arms to fall trapping the boys between them. A bell goes and the Professor rushes back on the stage. The boys are released and the Professor drags them to the centre of the stage where he reprimands them both for their dishonest action.

This is where the boys' play ended. Alternative endings could be tried, for example:

Since the boys are so anxious to make money, the Professor says that, to make amends, they can work for him for the rest of the day. It so happens he needs a lifting and pushing machine to improve the process. They are fitted in to the machine line up and, to their dismay, they have to work very hard without stopping. (Black-out as work continues.)

## CONCLUSION

So, quite rightly, in my opinion, some children and their teacher have been given the privilege of the last word in this collection of suggestions for drama. My hope is that at any rate some of these ideas will be of use, and better still, spark off others of your own. Let there be more purposeful doing of Drama in our schools. Having filled a book with words, may I now urge action.

A man of words and not of deeds
Is like a garden full of weeds;
And when the weeds begin to grow
It's like a garden full of snow;
And when the snow begins to fall,
It's like a bird upon the wall;
And when the bird away does fly,
It's like an eagle in the sky;
And when the sky begins to roar,
It's like a lion at the door;
And when the door begins to crack,
It's like a stile across your back,
And when your back begins to smart,
It's like a penknife in your heart;
And when your heart begins to bleed,
You're dead and dead, and dead indeed.

Anon

## BOOK REFERENCES

1. In *The Times*, Saturday, 4 January 1969
2. William Martin and Gordon Vallins, 'Journal 1665' in *Exploration Drama*, Evans
3. H. Grieve, *The Great Tide*, Essex Record Office
4. 'The Little Ark' in J. Britton, *Oxford Book of Stories for Juniors*, O.U.P.
5. 'The Great Stone Fire Eater' in *Folk Tales of all Nations*, ed. F. H. Lee, Harrap 1931
6. E. Power, 'Marco Polo' in *Medieval People*, Methuen
7. *The Travels of Marco Polo*, Penguin, pp. 6–7
8. M. S. Collis, *Marco Polo*, Faber & Faber, pp. 23–24
9. *Ibid* pp. 24–25
10. *Ibid* Chapters 6 and 7
11. *The Travels of Marco Polo*, Penguin, pp. 184–95, 207–8
12. Sonia Bleeker, *The Sioux*, Dobson
13. Sonia Bleeker, *The Inca Indians of the Andes*, Dobson
14. E. Hyams and G. Ordish, *The Last of the Incas*, Longmans
15. Harrington, *Dickon among the Indians*, Penguin
16. S. Gwynn, *Life of Mary Kingsley*, Penguin, 1932, Chapters 1 and 2
17. *Ibid*, pp. 72–3
18. *Ibid*, pp. 65–6
19. J. R. Ullman, *Man of Everest*, Harrap
20. Ronald W. Clark, *Great Moments of Rescue*, J. M. Dent
21. Bernard Newman, *The World of Espionage*, Souvenir Press
22. *The Travels of Marco Polo*, trs. R. Latham, Penguin, 1958
23. *James Watt*, Jackdaw Publications
24. Elizabeth Gaskell, *The Life of Charlotte Brontë*, 1919, pp. 85–7, Dent
25. Charlotte Brontë, *Shirley*, Chapters 19 and 22, Dent
26. M. B. Synge, *A Book of Discovery*, Nelson, Chapter 1
27. Bertolt Brecht, 'The Life of Galileo' in *Plays by Bertolt Brecht*, vol 1, Methuen, 1960
28. *Ibid*, sc.1
29. *Ibid*, sc.10
30. *Ibid*, sc.13
31. *Ibid*, sc.14